List of Contents

The author has received support from the Northern Ireland Community Relations Council which promotes a pluralist society characterised by equality, respect for diversity and interdependence. The views expressed do not necessarily reflect those of the Community Relations Council.

If Stones Could Speak

On the wall of the porch of St Columbs Cathedral in Londonderry is the foundation stone of that beautiful building that reads: 'If stones could speak, then London's praise should sound, who built this church and city from the ground.'

It tells of the commitment and devotion of a group of London companies who financed the building of that city and church in the early 1600s. It was finally completed in 1633 at a cost of £3,400 and dedicated as both a church and cathedral, the first Protestant church built since the Reformation.

Standing on its hilltop site from that date, St Columbs has existed through siege, World Wars, and civil conflict, never flinching from its function of service to the community and to God.

Despite damage from bomb and bullet during the famous siege of 1688 and through acts of terrorism of the 1980s, the Cathedral has remained as a place of sanctuary and solace, and through the years has continued in the service for which it was built, providing a centre of worship and peace for a beleaguered community.

During those years from its construction the names of many famous men and women from history have been included in its annals for both service and individual deeds of heroism. Names of those Siege heroes such as Captain Michael Browning and Governor George Walker are revered on tablet and recorded within its portals.

Hymn writers like Cecil Frances Alexander are remembered in perpetuity through stained glass and photograph for her work in promoting the Christian teachings in song and poetry. Her efforts for the poor and the ill are also recorded in the buildings vast records of the life of the city itself.

Dotted around the walls are memorials to other lesser-known individuals who also made their mark on society both locally, and in other corners of the world, and whose efforts were no less appreciated by all those who benefited from their existence.

Housed in that magnificent building the names gain the recognition they deserve because of their situation as well as for the acts of courage and selflessness noted on them.

Elsewhere in Northern Ireland there are also memorials to other men and women of courage who would receive no less recognition nor would be out of place if their names or acts of heroism were to be included in the Cathedral. Their memorials are in the many cemeteries and churches throughout this Province; their names bear testimony to their courage and selfless devotion to their country and fellow countrymen.

Theirs is not the controversial memorial that attempts to validate acts of terrorism, but a dignified and modest record that reminds us all that those who lost their lives as a result of terrorism, murdered at their homes, places of work, or going to church, did not deserve their fate. These men and women were not simply the statistics or numbers that the years and lack of interest by Government would indicate, but real live human beings who loved and were loved in return.

These stories are so easily forgotten in the continual propoganda of the terrorist programme who would have us believe that those whom they murdered were the enemies of this country. These are stories that, when told by those who loved them and who still love them, are ones of courage and humanity that cannot be etched on marble headstones and are the true reflection of these individuals who are not merely statistics of the terrorist war.

It is right that their sacrifice should be remembered, not only as names on a cold slab of marble but as fathers, husbands, wives, daughters, brothers and sisters, who gave their lives in the cause of freedom and to whom we should remain indebted and speak of with pride.

From the many gravestones around Northern Ireland, these are only some of the stories they would tell, if these stones could speak.

Where Eagles Fly

Let your thoughts fly
Let your hearts soar
Higher,
And higher
Where the eagles fly

Until
In the silence
You find peace
And you know
Who you are.

You've taken our land
We've died at your hand
You've taken our homes away
But while we still live
Our spirit will give
The strength for the fight to stay.

For here we belong
Our spirit is strong
It soars like a song in the sky
Defeat we'll deny
Our spirit won't die
It flies where the eagles fly.

• • •

From 'On Eagle's Wing' by John Anderson

Preface

In writing this book it has been necessary to travel to all parts of Northern Ireland to talk with some of those relatives who have lost loved ones during the murder years of the terrorist campaign in our country.

In doing so I have visited places I had never been before and saw countryside which is breathtaking in its beauty and people who I never knew before but who were warm and welcoming and above all were among the most courageous that I have ever met.

My excuse for not seeing the places before was that during the years of 'the troubles', unless it was absolutely necessary, no one made a journey to areas that could lead them inadvertently into danger that was either perceived or real.

The reason for meeting with those people I had heard about in news reports but in most instances had never actually met, was that they had stories to tell, stories that had been glanced over by the media when their loved ones had hit the headlines for a day following their murder.

In the carnage that filled those years since the nineteen seventies, death was an almost daily occurrence and a community shocked and numbed by the number of atrocities could not fully comprehend or digest the hurt and loss suffered by so many of their fellow countrymen.

Sadly, and disgracefully so, the loss was also mainly ignored by successive British Governments who have only paid lip service to the sacrifice of these men and women who served their country and Government policy by giving their lives.

In some instances that sacrifice was repaid by the Government of the day with a payment of as little as £70 to their family dependents and with the disbandment of forces in which they served.

For years those who have been left behind have all but been ignored by Central Governments and have carried their pain in silence with only themselves and their friends to remember the loss they have suffered.

While the perpetrators of the murders have in cases been glorified in public memorials, these individuals have almost been forgotten as history recedes into the past but the pain remains.

This book would not have been possible without the assistance and support of a number of people, some of whom I have only met for the first time but I now call friends and to them I want to say a sincere thanks.

Firstly, to the relatives of those whose stories are told in this book and for their courage, despite the lingering pain, in reliving a past that should never have happened. Their dignity and faith are above measure.

To Jean Long and the News Letter for showing an interest in what was happening and helping to tell another side of the history of the terror campaign.

Thanks also to Shelley Gilfillan for her excellent local knowledge and for making so many arrangements for me and therefore saving lots of time, as well as for her patience with all the telephone calls.

My thanks also to Neil Fenn for his help in emergency situations and his ability to come up with the goods when panic had set in. He is good to know.

Finally, to my friend Michael Clark for his patience, support and typing skills and especially for the long hours he sat at a keyboard and in a car driving across Northern Ireland. Thanks too for his directional and research abilities. He is an American with a heart that is a true Ulster Scot.

Each and Every Day

The sun came up and you awoke, you did not know what the
day ahead would bring, but those who ordered your death
and executed you, knew. I wish I could have changed their
minds, but that's what life brought us that day.

The sun it rises and I awake,
I started another day not knowing,
What life has in store for me,
But that's life.
You are gone, but your essence remains with us,
I wish I could have changed that day and
Then life would not be this way for me.

The sun has risen for me since that day
And I awake.
I miss you still and I always will,
But each day I try my best to make a difference
In the lives of those who suffer still.
I look to a future where no one else will die like you
And no one else will suffer like I do.

● ● ●

Written by Janet Hunter
Sister of Joseph McIlwaine

Bill Baggley
29 November 1931 – 29 January 1974

Bill Baggley was born an only child in Lincoln on 29 November 1931 and, after spending all of his young life there or in the small English village where his family moved to, he eventually joined the Royal Navy to make a career for himself.

His postings eventually brought him to Londonderry for a period and it was there at a dance in the Criterion Ballroom that he met the woman who was to be his wife. After a courtship of approximately 18 months, he and his bride, the former Joan Alford, were married in Glendermott Parish Church on 17 December 1955.

It was a perfect wedding and, indeed, a happy marriage, and one that was eventually blessed with the first of three children, a daughter whom they called Linda.

'Bill was the perfect family man and, having been an only child himself, he loved the fact that I was one of ten children myself; he certainly enjoyed the involvement it brought with all of my brothers and sisters with whom he got on extremely well,' said Joan.

'When we were first married he was transferred to various parts of the world, including the Antarctic, for many months at a time and, not having a permanent base, it was more sensible that I stayed on at home in Londonderry while he was away. In 1963 he was posted to Gibraltar for three years; by this time we had our second daughter and the four of us moved there during his time of service,' she said.

Their time in Gibraltar was the longest they had together during those early years and, while she enjoyed the experience, both were delighted when they got the opportunity to return to Northern Ireland, that by this time Bill was starting to accept as his own country. He was to be based at HMS Caroline in Belfast and the couple took the opportunity to buy their first family home together since their marriage.

'We bought a bungalow in 1962 and moved into it and were delighted with it. It was a new house and we worked to make it our home and I feel that we were very successful. Bill had to spend time in Belfast but there was something comforting in the fact that he was able to come home instead of living in married quarters, and we were certainly very happy,' recalled Joan.

'He was a great family man and a great provider for his family, their needs always came first and he was devoted to the two girls. Whenever he was going to the nearby shop, or just a walk, he took them with him; in fact, one neighbour once said to me that he always looked so proud when he walked up the street with them, and he was never seen without them by his side. They were equally devoted to him and I have to say that they would have gone with him before they would have gone out with me but I never minded.'

Joan still recalls the times that Bill had to leave to go to wherever he was based at a particular time and said that he always ensured that their needs were taken care of in his absence.

'I remember that when he had to leave to go back to whatever base he was in at the time, he always made sure that he took care of everything he could for us before he left. He was always thinking ahead and making sure that he had taken care of as much as he could for us before he went.'

Bill Baggley was never happier than when he was at home with his wife and children and eventually his third child, a son, was born and his family and happiness was complete.

'He was very family orientated, happy and content spending time with us, and his family was very important to him and nothing was too much trouble for him when it concerned his children,' said Joan. 'As a person Bill had very high standards in his life, he disliked lies and would never swear or use foul language in the house or in front of the children. Maybe he did when he was at work with the other men but I never heard him. He was always very careful in his conversations in front of us.'

In 1971 his service was complete with the Royal Navy and there was no hesitation in deciding what he was going to do. He was staying in Northern Ireland as he had grown to love it here over the years. 'He really did have a great affinity for Northern Ireland, he loved the country, the way of life and the people and, despite the Troubles, he never felt threatened as he had time for everyone.'

And so it was that Bill found work with the Ministry of Defence and settled down to civilian life with his wife and children whom he watched grow and flourish. He was happy with his lot in life.

'We eventually bought a car as he was now at home permanently and we were able to take days away and visit other members of my family who lived outside the town. We had many happy times and, with the children getting bigger, things were easier all around. Despite what was going on in the country, we were content in our own little world,' said Joan.

'Of course, we were like everyone else and cared what was happening and the number of innocent people who were being murdered, almost on a daily basis at that time. I remember when relatives were asked afterwards how they felt about the killers of their loved ones, I was often puzzled at the response of those who said that they could forgive those who had committed the murder. I often wondered how they could forgive, but it wasn't something that haunted me.'

By late 1973 Bill decided that he wanted to do something to serve his adopted country and decided that he would join the Royal Ulster Constabulary Reserve.

'I didn't have any real worries about his decision as I knew that he would be stationed in the Waterside area of Londonderry and most of the murders were happening in other parts of the country, and all of the troubles were on the other side of the bridge on the city side of the town. Apart from that, I knew that Bill was genuine in his reasons for joining and it was his love of his country that had made him decide to join the police.'

On Tuesday 29 January 1974 the day began as normal, children going to school, meals to be made, and work to go to. Joan had taken a job as a domestic in Altnagelvin Hospital to supplement the family income and to cater for the increasing needs of her growing children.

It was three weeks away from Linda's seventeenth birthday; as Joan started work at 5.30 p.m. Linda was able to look after the younger two as their father was also going on duty at 7.00 p.m.

'There was nothing unusual about that day. Bill drove me to work as he often did and said that he would see me when he got home. I would be home before he returned just after midnight and I would wait for him as usual.'

When she returned home from her work, Joan saw the children off to bed and sat in her living room reading a book while she waited for her husband. In the distance she heard the sirens of an ambulance going along the main road near her house, but as she lived near the hospital and sirens were a regular occurrence every day, she paid little or no attention.

'When Bill didn't get home at his usual time I didn't pay too much attention as I thought that there was a need for him to stay on or that he had given some colleague a lift home,' she said.

At ten minutes to one in the morning there was a knock at her front door and, when she opened it, there were two policemen standing there.

'At first they told me that there had been an accident and, as I listened, I still didn't realise fully what had happened and, even when they said that there had been a shooting, it still didn't register with me what they were trying to say. It was only when they said that Bill was dead that the whole thing hit me and after that I don't remember very much.'

Just before midnight Bill and a colleague were returning to the police station in Spencer Road, in the Waterside, at the end of their tour of duty and were only yards away from it when a gunman or gunmen shot both of the men in the back.

Bill Baggley died instantly and his colleague was seriously injured but recovered and lived for another five years before dying from cancer. The gunman was never caught.

'I don't remember much after the news was given to me, but I remember Linda standing in the hallway in her pyjamas and, looking back, I think that after she heard what she did, I feel that was the time that she decided that she was going to join the police herself. I remember the house filling up with friends and family as the news spread, but apart from that I don't remember very much. All I could think was that Bill was gone and would not be coming back. I dreaded to think how I was going to manage or go on without him as he was the centre of all our lives.'

Tragically, like so many others, Joan's life was torn apart that night and the person who would have been there to help her through was the very person she couldn't have but needed the most. With the help of those around her the days passed but the realisation of what had happened began to settle in as the shock gave way to grief.

'From the word go, the RUC were a great help and stayed with me from day one. They gave me first class support and I will be eternally grateful to them for all of their help when I needed it most,' she said.

When the time came for Bill's funeral it was attended by hundreds of people, but for Joan it was a complete blur. 'I can't remember anything about that day, it was afterwards when I looked at all of the newspaper cuttings that I saw Bill's funeral for myself and could read what happened. I was too overcome to notice anything for myself that day.'

Bill was laid to rest in the cemetery near the church in which he was married and where other of his colleagues are also buried after losing their lives in similar vicious and cowardly attacks.

'People say that when you lose someone you love that part of you goes with them and that is very true. When Bill died a big part of me died with him and that has never come back to me.'

In the months after his death Joan fought hard to cope with life without him and she admits herself that there were times when she wished that she had gone with him.

'It was really hard to manage without him, he was a big part of my life and there was a very big space without him. I had to be strong for the sake of our children and it was for their sakes that I felt I had to carry on. Sometimes I thought that if I sold the house we lived in and moved somewhere else then that would help to take the pain away, but this was his home and I stayed where I was. I am glad that I did as I know now that you only take the memories with you.'

In the thirty-one years since his murder, Joan has often reminisced on her life with him and how it could have been. 'Unfortunately the conclusion is always the same, Bill is not with me anymore, at least not physically, but I have wonderful memories of him.'

When asked how she felt about forgiveness for the person or persons who murdered him, Joan said that she had never contemplated forgiveness at all.

'The anger has lessened but the hurt is still very much there. One thing that I do know is that I was very proud of him, proud of his outlook, proud of his commitment to life, his family, and to Northern Ireland, and I still have that pride. He was more of a hero than the coward who had to come behind him to shoot him in the back.'

Sadly for Joan, this was not the end of her heartache and, just a few years later, tragedy struck her family again.

Linda Baggley
19 February 1957 – 2 June 1976

Linda Baggley's father was murdered three weeks before her seventeenth birthday and, despite her young years, she was a tremendous help to her mother in the days and months after his death. 'I would have to say that she was a great help and matured all of a sudden after her fathers death. She did whatever she could to make things as easy as possible for me and in our home,' said Joan.

'Thoughtful', 'obliging', and 'friendly' are words used often to describe Linda when her family or friends spoke of her and, in researching this story, many friends did speak glowingly of the young woman that they felt privileged to have as a friend.

'Linda loved music and the fashion of the time; her great idol was David Cassidy and she loved his singing and music,' said her mother. 'She had lots of friends and very often, when some of them called for her, I could hear them laughing and talking outside the front door. She was quite popular.'

Academically, too, Linda did very well and Joan recalls one particular parents evening at her school when her form master was talking about her. 'He said that he had no problems at all with Linda's school work, but that she spent a lot of time gazing out of the window at the school playing fields, especially when the boys were out there playing football. What could I say about that? She was a typical young girl of her day and I suppose she was like many of her friends.'

In 1975 Linda told her mother that she was thinking of joining the police and although she had many reservations about her decision, Joan didn't say anything to stop her.

'I know that I couldn't have changed her mind but, to be honest, I didn't think she would be accepted as she wore glasses, and I felt this would not be acceptable. I also felt that after what had happened to her father they would not consider allowing her to enrol.'

That was not to be the case, however, and in July 1975, Linda became a member of the Royal Ulster Constabulary Reserve.

'When she told me that she had been accepted I have to admit that my stomach sank, but I didn't say anything to her, I knew that she really wanted to follow in her father's footsteps in whatever way she could and I couldn't stop her doing that.'

Initially she was stationed in Strand Road on the West Bank of the city and had to start work at 7.00 p.m. in the evenings. As she didn't finish her fulltime work until 6.00 p.m. it was a bit of a rush to get home, washed, changed, and across to work on time. I think that she must have asked for a transfer to the Waterside because of this but, anyway, that is where she ended up. She did a number of evening duties through the week and did some court duties every Tuesday and that's the way it continued for her.'

That was the way it went for some months and, although Joan still worried about her, she accepted that this was what her daughter wanted to do. On the night of Sunday 23 May 1976

Linda was getting ready for duty as usual and went through her usual routine, but not in such a rush this time.

'She had long hair which she put up when in uniform but, when she was travelling to work, she kept it down. That was her main concern that night and she wanted to know if it looked alright. When she was reassured that it was she set off and I saw her as she walked down the street past the window.'

Later that night some of Joan's family visited her at the house as they had done since Bill was murdered and there was also a friend of her other daughter there as well. At approximately 10.30 p.m. there was a knock at the door and the daughter went to answer it.

'I went out to the hall as well and, when the door was opened, there were two policemen standing there, both very ashen-faced. I think I knew right away what had happened and I just walked back into the living room where everyone else was sitting. They explained to me that Linda had been shot but that they would take me to the hospital to see her and, because they said that, it gave me some hope and I went with them.'

When they arrived at the hospital, it was explained to Joan that Linda was being prepared for surgery, as it was felt she had a broken jaw. 'She was heavily bandaged and was either unconscious or asleep, but I waited until I could see her when she was returned to the ward.'

Linda was on duty that evening with another colleague, Constable Ken Sheehan, when IRA gunmen ambushed them. Linda, who was unarmed, as woman constables did not carry weapons at this time, was shot at close range in the neck.

Constable Sheehan was shot several times and seriously injured and, after being in hospital for a long period, recovered and was so dedicated to his vocation that he returned to duty as soon as it was possible for him. He was transferred to Moneymore where he was tragically ambushed for a second time and died on 8 April 1977.

On Tuesday 25 May Linda was airlifted by helicopter to the Royal Victoria Hospital in Belfast as she needed specialist treatment, and her mother went with her.

'I had a sister who lived in Belfast so I went up to stay with her and my family in Londonderry looked after my two other children, my son would have been only seven years old at the end of the month. I travelled by car to Belfast as soon as I had made all the arrangements for the children and, when I arrived at the Royal Victoria Hospital, Linda was in the Intensive Care Unit and had been connected to a ventilator to help her breathe.'

Joan stayed most of her time in Belfast with her daughter and only took breaks when others came to visit, and Linda had many visitors. 'Lots of her friends and my family came to see her as well as many of her colleagues in the police. She never woke at all when they were there, but I know she would have appreciated their visits; I know that I certainly did. The police were very supportive and attentive, and for all their help, I am very grateful.'

Joan had asked if it would be possible for her son to visit, but was advised against it by the surgeon, even when it was explained to him how close Linda and her brother were. Instead, he asked Joan whenever he saw her if her son had been told about Linda, and when he was told that he had not, he said that it would be better if he were and that it should be Joan who told him. 'He said it every time he saw me and maybe he was trying to tell me something then but I either missed it or didn't want to hear what he was saying to me.'

In the end, after having been in Belfast a week, Joan decided that she would pay a visit back home to give whatever reassurance she could to the other children and, if possible, explain to her son what had happened.

On one of her visits to Linda the nurse had explained that they had taken Linda off the ventilator for a while, but had to replace it again and that Linda was 'a fighter'. Pleased at what she heard, Joan went back home for the night on Tuesday 1 June and did get the opportunity to talk to her son and explain to him what had happened. He was just seven but, while he asked lots of questions, he accepted what he was told.

Intending to return to Belfast the next day she spent that night with her children and the next day rose early to pack a new bag for her return to her injured daughter. 'The phone rang at eight thirty and it was the hospital to ask me to come. A police driver came for me and we set off shortly after the call.'

On the way to the Royal there was a detour due to a bomb scare, and while they had made good time on their journey, there was a slight delay in reaching their destination. 'Linda had already died by the time I got there and I didn't have the chance to be with her.'

Outside the hospital on the same day, Detective Constable Ronald McAdam was shot dead by the IRA as he waited to collect a friend. He was off duty at the time of his murder.

Just like her father before her, Linda was buried with full police honours after a service in her parish church. She was laid to rest with her father having been shot just yards from where he himself had been murdered.

'People said to me that the worst thing that could happen was to lose a child and I know what they mean. I found her death particularly hard, I still find it hard. Nevertheless, I think she was very brave and I am very proud of her. Linda was unarmed when she was shot at close range. She is more the hero than the coward who shot her.'

Alan Smyth

29 March 1954 - 24 April 1994

Alan Smyth was the oldest of a family of five and, although he wouldn't admit it, he held a special place in his mother's affections. In fact, his younger brothers and sister used to tease her about it.

'We know she had no favourites but she had that extra bond with Alan and, though none of us minded, we would often make fun with her about it,' said his younger brother Dessie.

'Alan was very easygoing in his manner and would have done anything for anyone and, though he had many close friends, he was very quiet in nature. He was no softie, however, and when necessary he could certainly hold his own and give a good account of himself.'

At six-feet-one-inch tall and very strong, Alan was an imposing figure, but he had a soft centre when it came to children.

'He never had any children of his own but he spoiled all his nephews and nieces something rotten. When they were at the house they used to ask him if he was going into the town and, even if he wasn't going in, he would take them and buy them whatever they wanted.'

Alan was born on 29 March 1954 near the little village of Garvagh in County Londonderry; he had an abiding love of football and of Glasgow Rangers in particular, his favourite team.

'While he never played the game himself, he loved watching and would often travel to Scotland to see them and bring back presents for all the children. Apart from his football he played a few games of darts or snooker with his friends but, with working all week, he restricted his socialising to mostly weekends. He would have a drink then but never on a Sunday or on any night that he was working the following day,' said Dessie.

In the late 1970s, like so many other young men and women, Alan decided he would like to do something to serve his country and so became a part-time member of the Ulster Defence Regiment.

While he still carried on his fulltime work as a security officer, he gave up his evenings to go and patrol with his colleagues in an effort to help stop the terrorist campaign that was being waged at the time.

By the early '80s he decided to join fulltime and gave up his general employment to devote more time to this form of security, which he felt benefited the whole of the community.

'He stayed in it for a number of years until he found another fulltime job and finally handed in his uniform, feeling that he had done his bit.'

During his time in the Regiment Alan drove to work one morning, just as other members of his family did, and was contacted some time later to be told that an explosive device had been found on the road leading from their home.

'Alan and another brother had the same type of car and it is unknown which car the bomb was attached to, but by luck it had fallen off and neither one of them was hurt.'

Even after he left the UDR Alan was still seen as a target for the terrorists and on St Patrick's Day 1993 he had driven to his new job as usual and got out of the car to go inside.

'Just as he went inside his work the car exploded and burst into flames. It seems that a mercury tilt device had been placed under it and, somehow or other, it didn't explode until then. There were others travelling with him at the time and everyone could have been killed.'

Afterwards, none of his workmates would accept a lift because of their fear of another bomb; Alan travelled alone from then on.

'It was around that time that I suggested to him that he should move to England for a while and stay with some family that we had over there, but he refused. He just said that they would not scare him out of his own country and that he wasn't afraid of them.'

Just a few months before his murder, Alan's father died and it was Dessie who had to go to the hospital to make a formal identification of his body.

'He had been having trouble with his heart which seemed to happen all of a sudden as he was a big strong man who worked hard all his life. When he was having surgery to repair it, his aorta burst and he died in the operating theatre.'

It was a terrible blow to the family, and especially to their mother, who was devastated at the loss of her husband and, like all the family, Alan gave her as much support as possible.

'I remember him saying to her that now our father was dead that he would look after her in his place and, while he was alive, he did.'

For several years the family had been getting anonymous telephone calls and it was their mother, in particular, who was the target.

"When we were out in the evenings someone would ring the house and tell my mother that two of her sons wouldn't be coming back that night and she used to keep asking, who is this and why are you doing it? They went on for a long time and we often told her just to hang up when they came but we know it worried her.'

There was one other time when Alan was parked on the main street in Garvagh when a well-known republican was being driven past by another man in a car. When he saw Alan, he made his finger and thumb into the form of a gun, his finger being the barrel, and pointed towards him and pretended to shoot before they drove off.

Some time later Alan saw the two in a fish and chip shop and went inside to remind the man what he had done when he last drove past. He suitably chastised both and he came away satisfied that it would not be happening again.

Sunday 24 April passed like many others in the Smyth household and, by the afternoon, everyone was making arrangements for what they were doing that evening.

'I was going to Coleraine with my girlfriend to visit her brother in the hospital there and Alan was going to collect his lifelong friend and spend some time in the town. I left the house about ten past five and he said that he would see me later. That was the last time I saw him alive.'

When Dessie was leaving the hospital after his visit at approximately ten minutes to seven, he saw an ambulance rushing into the Accident and Emergency department. He happened to notice a policewoman standing up over whoever the patient was inside.

'I remember saying at the time that there must have been an accident but I never suspected for a moment how it was going to turn out.'

Earlier that evening Alan had collected his friend and the two of them were parked on the main street in Garvagh. It was just after six in the evening and some people were walking down the street to attend the evening service in the Presbyterian Church.

One of those who was on his way was another friend of Alan's, a young man by the name of John McCloy. He had just called into the shop opposite to where Alan was parked and, when he saw Alan and his other friend, he went over to talk with them.

John's parents were also on the street walking on their way to church, while John had come in his car.

'It was the car that the friends were talking about as John leaned in the window and Alan had suggested buying it from him. They had come to an agreement and were about to shake on it but John said no as it was not lucky to make deals on a Sunday.'

Suddenly there was a screech of brakes and a car ground to a halt in front of them … bullets were being fired from automatic weapons.

When the shooting stopped, the car sped off, leaving Alan seriously injured but still alive. His friend was also injured and it was he who was taken in the ambulance that Dessie saw at the hospital.

John McCloy who had just stopped for a quick chat with his friends was also dead and, despite his injuries, when he saw his friend was dead, Alan's last words were: 'O no, not John.'

People ran to help the dead and injured and Alan lived for twenty minutes after the shooting, before succumbing to his injuries. 'He had been hit a few times in the chest and abdomen but, with all of this, he still survived for that twenty minutes.'

The killer jumped back into the car he had come from and sped out of Garvagh towards the village of Kilrea and, fortunately, ran into a UDR patrol that had been in the area who immediately arrested all the occupants. The killer was tried and convicted and ordered to serve two life sentences for the murder of the two men, fortunately the third survived.

While serving his sentence he reportedly escaped from prison dressed as a woman, but he has subsequently been released under the terms of the Good Friday Agreement.

On the day of his funeral, Alan was buried at 11.00 in the morning and John at 2.00 in the afternoon. Between fifteen hundred and two thousand people attended the funerals.

Despite the huge support, however, it did not diminish the heartache of her loss for Alan's mother.

'I know that for a long while afterwards she found it hard to accept that he was dead and would not be coming home. It took a long time for the hurt to heal in her.'

At one stage she said to Dessie that Alan had promised to look after her after his father had died, but now that was impossible.

In Dessie's opinion, and that of many in the same situation, the so-called peace process is 'a complete farce'; it is the families who have become the forgotten victims.

'When this individual escaped he was then freed under the terms of the Good Friday Agreement. No one even felt it necessary to tell us that he had escaped; it was only when a newspaper called to ask what my mother thought of the news that we found out. It's as if we didn't matter at all.'

David Pollock
24 October 1960 - 20 October 1990

The one great love of David Pollock's life was motorcars and motorbikes and, from the time he was able to drive, he bought and exchanged cars the way other young people bought shirts.

'He was forever changing his car and getting a different one that had something on it that appealed to him,' recalls his sister Catherine. 'He just loved them and loved to drive.'

David was one of a family of eight children and was 'the life and soul of the household'.

'He was great fun and a great practical joker that seemed to be always on the go, you just couldn't hold him down,' she said.

He was born on 24 October 1960 in the little County Tyrone village of Artigarvan and, even as a young boy, was very good when it came to working with his hands.

'When it came to schooling I would have to say that he just tolerated it and couldn't wait until he was the age when he could leave and begin working,' said his mother Kathleen. 'He became a joiner by trade and was very good at it, he made units for the house for me and even did our first extension at the back of the house. David was very helpful and obliging.'

On entering his working life, his first job was with a nearby firm making portakabins and from there he moved on to a number of other jobs, always bettering himself in the process.

In the late 1970s, David gave up his joinery work and enlisted in the 6th Battalion of the Ulster Defence Regiment and was stationed not far from his home at Burndennett.

Time with them passed uneventfully for him and five years later he decided that he was ready for a change and resigned to start a different type of work, this time at a local creamery.

With this job he had to do shift work but this gave him more time for his main passion of motorcars, and David settled back into civilian life very easily.

For the next seven years he carried on with his work at the creamery and lived his life quietly with his lifelong passion for cars still taking up much of his time, and doing all the things that young men did at that time. There was no indication at all of the horror that was to come.

Saturday 20 October 1990 was just three days away from his thirtieth birthday and he was on one of his days off work. It was just another day for the family with everyone going through their normal routine.

David had been in and out of the house all day doing various bits and pieces and, being his normal self, was talking and laughing as usual.

He had arranged to visit his girlfriend that evening in the nearby village of Sion Mills and had agreed to drop one of his sisters and a friend of hers at a nearby bar.

'You had to be ready on time if you were going out with David as he was extremely punctual; he left the house exactly at the time he wanted,' said Catherine. 'He had agreed to give me and one of my friends a lift that night and, as usual, he was ready before any of us.'

He dropped his sister and friend off at their destination and continued towards his girlfriend's home and, to get to it, he had to pass through the county town of Strabane. He had been on the road many times and it was second nature to him, and to his family, that he would be taking the same well-travelled route.

'We never felt we had to worry about David at all as he had been out of the UDR so long that we had even forgotten that he had been in it,' said Catherine.

Unfortunately, others had not forgotten and, despite the fact that he had only recently changed his car again, someone knew the type that he would be driving and there was an ambush waiting for him along the road.

'When he was driving along the Melmount Road, near Melmount Chapel, a car came driving towards him and swerved into his path. It hit the drivers side of David's car and pushed him off the road.'

The occupants then jumped out and shot David between four and five times. His death certificate shows that he had a 'laceration of the heart and had been hit on the left lung and liver'.

When they finished shooting, they hijacked a passing car and ordered the disabled driver and child out of it before driving off.

'I think that David must have been knocked unconscious when the car hit him as otherwise he would have got out and ran as he was very much into keep fit,' said Catherine. 'As it was he had no way of defending himself.'

Worshippers were just leaving the nearby church after Mass and, on hearing the shooting, some ran to help David, but despite their efforts there was nothing that anyone could do to help him.

However, some witnesses were able to identify the killers and gave descriptions and other information to an army patrol that had arrived on the scene. The patrol went immediately to the address given and was able to apprehend the three-man gang who still had the weapons they had just used to murder the unarmed young man.

His mother Kathleen was at home when her son was murdered and was told about it when the police came to the house with a minister from the nearby Church of Ireland Church with the dreadful information.

Like so many other mothers, she was devastated at the loss of her son and admits that the house is still empty without him.

'I had to try and get on with my life for the sake of the others, but there are many things that I miss about him, things that others might think silly but things that I knew was David. I remember when he was on early shifts he would poke the fire about a quarter past six in the morning and I could hear it upstairs, that's the sort of thing I still think about. There are many things which showed his presence in the house that don't happen now, and the house is quieter without him. I am glad that those who did it were caught,' she said.

The three men who were sentenced for the murder of David Pollock were William Alphonsus Patrick McAteer, Thomas John Brennan, and Seamus Matthew McGarrigle, all from Strabane. All were sentenced to long terms in prison but have been released under the terms of the Good Friday Agreement.

Jillian Johnston
17 April 1966 - 18 March 1988

Jillian Johnston was born into a loving family, the fifth in a family of six children who lived in the townland of Tonaghgorm, Leggs, between Belleek and Kesh in County Fermanagh. It was an idyllic childhood for the young girl who was close to her other brothers and sisters as they grew up on their father's small farm with its panoramic views over Lough Erne.

In her early years she attended Kesh Primary School before moving on to the Duke of Westminster High School. She also enrolled for various part-time courses at Fermanagh College of Further Education.

During her early years she was a member of Pettigo Girls Brigade and on Sunday she supervised the taped music used at the little St John's Church of Ireland Parish Church at Muckross for worship. The church had no resident organist and very few members of a congregation due to the small number of Protestant families living in the area, so Jillian's efforts were necessary for congregational participation.

On leaving school, Jillian's first employment was in a car salesroom where she worked as a clerk for two years before moving to the medical records department of the Erne Hospital where she stayed for nine months. Her last place of work was as an assistant in a chemist in the village of Belleek and this was where she was still working at the time of her murder.

Described by her mother as a 'quiet, reserved girl' who had no interest in politics, but who loved her home and family and who also loved to go dancing in her spare time. In fact, it was at a dance at the Lough Erne Hotel in 1981 that she first met her fiancée, Stanley, who later said that from that meeting the two realised that they 'were meant for each other'.

'They were very happy and Stanley used to travel from County Tyrone, where he lived, to see Jillian as often as possible,' said her sister Jacqueline. When I got married I moved to Tyrone myself and Jillian used to come here to stay at weekends to be near Stanley.'

It was obvious to all who knew them that the young couple were happy together and eventually they became engaged with the hope of marriage in the near future, but that was never to be.

As Jacqueline recounted the story of her sister's last day it is still hard to believe, even after all these years, that three gunmen who knew absolutely nothing about her could decide that her life should be taken from her.

'Stanley had gone to collect Jillian from her work at the chemist shop and the two of them left there at approximately ten minutes past six. They drove home, had tea, and decided to stay in that evening and watch television.'

That is what the young couple did for the early part of the evening but, around half past nine, they decided to drive to a café in Belleek and buy some fish and chips. Because it was raining, Stanley parked outside and left Jillian in the car while he ran inside to buy what they wanted, and when he had done so, they drove to the main street and sat there while they ate their purchases. While they ate they discussed the arrangements for the wedding they were planning and which they hoped to share with their families in the next few days.

By this time the couple had been going out together for six years and had been engaged for two of them. The wedding had been planned for the little church where Jillian had played so active a role and where she had been such a regular attendee and where the teachings had led Jillian to become a born again Christian.

Stanley did some farming himself and, because his sheep were close to lambing, he wanted to get home early that night, so when they had finished eating they set off again so that he could leave Jillian home.

Before they had first left the house some neighbours of theirs had answered a knock at the door to their home at twenty minutes to nine and, when they opened it, two men forced their way inside. Describing what happened in some newspaper reports at the time, the lady of that house said that the two men had, '… black hoods and green and brown jackets, the same as the army wear. They both carried long guns and told us to stay where we were.'

Her husband said that the men had also taken the keys to their car and that he was too frightened to look out of the house after they had gone. 'I gave them the keys, what else could I do? They both had guns, they were black rifles.'

The couple said that the gunmen left their home at a quarter past ten and didn't know anything of the events that happened later until their son called them at a quarter past nine the next morning when he had heard about the murder. Ignorant of what had happened at the neighbour's house, the two young people drove back along the county roads and turned into the long drive which led to Jillian's home, and when they reached the yard, Stanley was about to reverse the car to turn it when the shooting started.

All the young man could remember was seeing a number of flashes and hearing loud bangs. After that he remembers calling for help and then waking up in hospital suffering from serious wounds.

Inside the house her mother was at home on her own and she remembers hearing the car arriving in the yard and then hearing some bangs which she said seemed to go on and on.

Petrified with fear, she sat in shock and, while she adjusted to the terror of what she had just experienced, Jillian's mother heard the killers walk past the window of the room where she was sitting. She could clearly hear the laughter as they talked of what they had just done, but she still was totally unaware of what had just happened to her beloved daughter.

'It was a quarter past ten and, although I heard the shooting, I never thought that they had come to shoot anyone. I was so afraid that I rang my sister-in-law to come over to me.'

However, she summoned the courage to go to the door when she heard Stanley's calls for help; she ran to the blue Ford Fiesta car that had been raked with bullets. 'I knew that Jillian was dead and Stanley was in great pain so I talked to him a minute and then ran back to the house to get help. I was heartbroken and terrified.'

Totally terrorised and stricken by grief, she kept running back and forth to the car while she waited for the much-needed help to arrive and all the while hoping that this was all a nightmare that would soon pass. 'I kept thinking that maybe Jillian would be alive when I went back to the car, but every time it was just the same sight that greeted me.'

At an inquest into her death the full horrific facts became known to everyone in her family, and the public. At least two gunmen had been involved with a third somewhere in the vicinity in the car they had stolen from the neighbours to help the assassins make their escape. They had probably hidden in nearby bushes while they waited for their targets and, while the car was reversing, they struck.

The spray of bullets ripped into the front and sides of the car and into the occupants who had no chance at all of defending themselves, and no reason at all of thinking they had to. Both were thrown around in their seats as the bullets hit their bodies and, in Jillian's case, the twenty bullets that hit her body left her lying against the passenger door. Stanley had multiple wounds to various parts of his body including his head but, thankfully, has recovered, at least in the physical sense.

According to the pathologist's report at the time, Jillian was hit twenty times by one group of high velocity bullets from behind and another from her left, and the bullets had all passed through the car before hitting her.

Instead of going to her wedding the family gathered with many hundreds of friends and well-wishers for her funeral in the little parish church where she had found the faith which raised her above the beliefs of her killers and which will bring her closer to the God she loved and accepted as her salvation. Following the service she was laid to rest in the adjoining cemetery.

In a statement over a week after the murder, the IRA accepted that their volunteers were responsible for her death, but that it had been a mistake, 'based on bad information which had been badly carried out'.

Sinn Fein President Gerry Adams described her death as 'unjustified and unjustifiable', but made no attempt to assist in bringing the perpetrators of this despicable act to justice.

This was not the only insult in the time after her death, the next coming two years afterwards when a letter arrived from the Northern Ireland Office offering £750 compensation to the family for their daughter's life. Some of the money was to pay for her funeral expenses and the rest to compensate for the lack of earnings coming into the house from Jillian since her murder.

This was calculated from the date of her death until the proposed date of her wedding.

Claiming that even had they made an offer of a million pounds it would not have compensated for the loss of her daughter's life. Her mother said that such an offer was 'an insult to us and to her memory'. Local Members of Parliament also condemned the offer, and that of other offers made to the members of other families in similar situations, and especially to the lack of follow-up support given to family members in such circumstances.

A year after the murder Jillian's family moved from the family home to another home where her mother felt 'safer' and where the memories would not be so vivid. 'The house was lonely and, while it was heartbreaking having to leave, it had to be done. We will not be giving it up altogether, but the memories are too hard.'

With the approach of the dark winter nights after the murder of her daughter, Jillian's mother found the fear unbearable and could no longer stay in the house in which her husband was brought up. She has since moved to a local village and a memorial has been erected to Jillian in the Parish Church. No one has ever been brought to justice for her murder.

Frederick John Lutton

24 August 1939 - 1 May 1979

The 'Murder Triangle' of Northern Ireland, as it became known, is an area comprised of East Tyrone and North Armagh. Along with the "Bandit country" of South Armagh, it saw many of the worst murders of the Troubles. The area was notorious during the '70s, '80s, and '90s as a zone where political and sectarian murders were almost a daily routine.

In many cases in both areas the Unionist and Loyalist perspective of the Republican campaign was that of ethnic cleansing – many of the murders carried out had no connections with the security forces but were simply the eradication of the Protestant population in the area.

For many Protestants, the legacy of that time is the loss of often more than one family member, and many children were left without a parent from the campaign of genocide.

One such child was Nigel Lutton who has vivid memories of the murder of his father Frederick when he was eight years old.

The family lived in the little village of Annaghmore, between Portadown and Dungannon in North Armagh, well within that infamous triangle.

'My father was a kind man who loved his family and loved working on the small farm that he had and where he raised beef cattle. He loved the open air and all things to do with nature, particularly wild life. I remember that he had a shotgun which he used to kill vermin such as rats, but he would never shoot a bird or a rabbit, and everyone used to pull his leg because of it.'

Eric was very much a family man and devout in his Christian faith. He was Churchwarden of Annaghmore Parish Church and a member of the Orange Order.

'I can never remember him swearing or raising his voice or hand to either myself or my young sister who was four years younger than me. When he told us to do something however, we did it, as we knew that he meant what he said. I never saw him smoking either and the only time he ever had a drink was at Christmas or on special occasions. He had been a member of the B Specials until they were disbanded and then he went on to join the Royal Ulster Constabulary Reserve,' said Nigel.

He had other happy memories too of his short time with the father he loved dearly but who was taken away from him so cruelly.

'I remember when he used to go out to the fields on the tractor that I would go with him and sit on the mudguard; we would have a great time together. Every day that I had off school would be spent with him.'

Along with the farm, Eric also had another job as estate manager at The Argory, a 200-year-old manor house, which is now the property of the National Trust, but at that time was owned by Mr Walter McGeough-Bond, the last of the family, who had built the estate.

'I used to go there with him as well when I was off school and Mr Bond used to make me very welcome. The estate was set in over 300 acres of lawns and woodland and it was great playing around there while my father worked. I remember him working at clearing a path from the house to the Blackwater Bridge that had become overgrown. Those memories are as vivid today as they were then and I think of those times often.'

Christmas too held special memories for the young boy and, in particular, the days leading up to it.

'For a week or so before Christmas Eve there was great excitement in the house, and I remember finding it difficult to sleep. For days leading up to it, my father would give me little toy animals like sheep or cows or whatever and say that I could have them if I was good and went to bed. Of course, I went to bed after the presents, and on Christmas morning what did I receive, but a whole farmyard including barns and everything else it needed to put the animals my father had given me into it.'

There were often debates in the house about bedtime, and with his sister being younger, it meant that she had to go to bed earlier, which she refused to do if her 'big' brother was allowed to stay up. It was agreed that if I went to bed at the same time as her that I could come back down when she had fallen asleep and stay up until about nine o' clock.

That was how it was on the last evening that Nigel shared with his father.

'When he came back from work that day he had called in at a local shop on his way home and bought me a toy tractor, and I remember being really pleased with it. He was always doing things like that for my sister and myself.

'That evening I went to bed as usual and, once my sister had fallen asleep, I came back downstairs and sat with him on the settee. We watched either The Professionals or The New Avengers together, I can't remember which, and then it was time for me to go back to bed. Before I went up he said my prayers with me and then gave me a hug and said good night. That was the last time that I ever saw him.'

The next morning Eric went off to work at The Argory and Nigel would have gone with him as he was off school for May Day, but for the fact that he slept in. There was nothing to tell anyone that this day would have been any different to the others and certainly no need to worry.

'Three weeks earlier he had left the Reserve police to take up a fulltime job as estate manager for the National Trust, so I don't think anything was on anyone's mind. A lot of people were being murdered and I remember hearing about two brothers being murdered in a factory near our home simply because they were successful Unionist businessmen, and there was the Tullyvallen massacre, where five Orangemen were murdered in their hall during the opening prayers. It was another example of the genocide of the Protestant people inside the "Murder Triangle".'

When he had finished his work for that day, Eric did what he normally did and went around the inside of the Argory to close all the wooden shutters, light the gas lights if necessary, and lock all the doors.

That particular night, the elderly Mr Bond had been feeling poorly and, as in similar instances when he was ill, Eric took him in the car to leave him in the local hotel where he would spend the night in comfort and be looked after.

When they reached the entrance gates to the estate, there was a car parked on the opposite side of the road from the entrance but, as it was a similar one to a friend of his, Eric had no reason to be alarmed or concerned about it.

As he normally did, he drove to the outside of the gates and got out to close them behind himself. Just when he turned his back to push the gates closed, two men got out of the car and shot him in the back. Eric was unarmed at the time and died on the way to hospital.

It later transpired that the car had been stolen and it was felt that it was chosen so that Eric would not show concern at its presence at the gates and their ambush would have a better chance of success.

When the gunmen fired they both returned to the car and drove off at high speed from the crime scene, but here there is a mystery.

Because of the number of murders in the area there had been an increase in security on the country roads and, further along the road that they took, there were two security checkpoints and neither one had seen the car or had it pass through, so how did the murderers make their escape?

'There is speculation, and a degree of justification for thinking, that the car drove into a cattle truck that was waiting for them just down the road and was ferried through by the driver as that was the only vehicle that had come past the checkpoints. I know that they could not have carried out the murder or escaped without some support from the local community,' said Nigel.

Because he was no longer a serving police officer, Eric was not entitled to a police funeral, but many of his colleagues attended the service in the church in uniform where Eric had been a member for many years.

'I miss my father and I miss the many years that I could have had with him. The IRA claimed his murder and so many others where I lived. I will never forgive them for what they did, and it turns my stomach to know that our British Government now wants us to concede to having terrorists in the Northern Ireland Assembly.

'I feel that the life that I should have had has been taken away from me and many of the times that should have been special to me have been denied to me as well. My father was only 39 when he died, he worked hard all of his life, and he did all he could for everyone in the community. I was a child of eight when he died and there are many years that I spent missing him and losing out on getting to know him more. I could never forget what they did to him or my family and, while I remember, I will never forgive.'

Being a child Nigel did not know what had happened or why, and he was never taught to hate; it was only in his teenage years that he began to have a fuller understanding of what was going on in his community.

'At the time of my father's death I saw a lot of coming and going in the house and I remember the sadness of knowing that I would never go out with him again or sit with him in the evenings. I can remember a policeman talking to my mother about what had happened and my mother wanted to put me out of the room but the policeman said: "He's only a child and he won't understand." I understood perfectly what he was saying and what had happened and that was the time that I started to really understand what was being done to my neighbours and their families.

'When I was sixteen I was taking more interest in what was happening around me, and I realised that many of our neighbours wanted us out of the area along with all the other Protestants. My mother stayed on and worked the farm for ten years after our father was killed, but she was unable to keep on doing it as it was too much for her. We sold it eventually to a good friend of the family.'

Since his father's death Nigel has worked unceasingly for other victims of terrorism and to have his father's name, and nineteen other ex-RUC officers in similar circumstances, included on the memorial at Brooklyn.

'Because he had left the police three weeks earlier it seems that he was not entitled to have his name recorded, but it was because he had served his community as a policeman that he lost his life in the first place. I felt that this was totally unjust as he and others like him had served their country proudly and paid the highest price possible for having done so. They had the same right to be remembered as the other men and woman who served with courage and who lost their lives for doing so.'

After a lot of canvassing and persuasion he has at last been successful in his quest and another plaque has been placed in the Memorial Garden with the names of those ex-policemen who were murdered as a result of service to the community.

'Now I am looking forward to their names being included in the Book Of Remembrance,' he said.

John McKeegan
8 May 1941 - 19 November 1981

When she was just fifteen years old Lila was out walking through the village of Donemana with a friend of hers. As they walked they met John McKeegan and a friend of his who were riding through the streets on their bicycles. The chance meeting led to the four young people stopping to talk and the end result was that John asked Lila for a date that following Tuesday afternoon which she accepted.

That date led to a long-term romance with the young man who was just a year older and, some years later on 9 October 1962, the young couple married in St James Parish Church in Donemana.

Their time together was idyllic and, one year after their wedding, they were blessed with the first of three children, a daughter. Eighteen months after her, their son arrived and, after him, their second daughter.

'They were very happy years, John was very kind hearted and generous and adored his children and every Friday night he brought me a bunch of flowers or a plant. I had taken a break from working as I wanted to spend time with the children until they had grown up,' said Lila.

Their years together were contented years and every season saw them using every opportunity they had to enjoy their family life together. 'In the autumn we used to gather nuts in the countryside just before Halloween and at Christmas everything was made special for the celebration. We always went to my family home for Christmas dinner in the old tradition and everything was wonderful.'

Both Lila and John worked together in a shirt factory and, after she took time out to care for their family, John still carried on working and providing for his family. 'He used to come home with his pay packet unopened and hand it to me as he always said that his family came first in his life.'

The couple eventually bought a caravan which they kept at the seaside town of Portrush, spending as much time there as possible. For them it became another world and far away from the Troubles that were raging back home and in the cities near them.

'We had a great time there as a family and could spend time together with no worries and in virtual safety.'

John by this time had changed jobs and was now working in a timber merchants in the nearby town of Strabane. He had been a member of the B Specials, a supplementary police force used primarily for guarding the border and special installations against terrorist attack. With the introduction of the Ulster Defence Regiment on 1 January 1970, the Specials became obsolete so he transferred to this newly-formed Regiment of the British Army who had the same task as their forerunners. He had initially applied to join the Royal Ulster Constabulary but, although he had passed the required entrance examination, he was turned down because he suffered from colour blindness.

'Although I felt uneasy I never tried to talk him out of it as this was what he wanted to do and I could understand his reasons. With his membership there were a lot of changes in their lives because of the security threat to the members of the regiment. Our social life changed as there were places we could not go, areas such as the town of Strabane became out of bounds for socialising and even shopping and we just had to accept it.'

For those reasons their caravan and times in Portrush became even more precious. They spent as much time there as possible and looked forward to the weekends when they could get away from everything. By the mid seventies the terror campaign was at its worst and every day brought news of another murder of a member of the security forces. Lila became more concerned about John's safety, more so when she had returned to work fulltime and stood at the bus stop to catch her transportation home.

'I looked across the road to a house in New Buildings where a young man who lived there had been murdered. I watched the lights in the house and thought how terrible and tragic it was and I worried more.'

She was so worried that she asked her husband to get a sick line from his doctor that would take him over Christmas, but he declined her suggestion and carried on with his job and with his security duties with the UDR. On the morning of 19 November everything was as normal in their home, both set off for their respective jobs in the expectation that they would meet up again in the evening, but that was not to be.

At ten minutes to two in the afternoon, Lila's floor manager called to her that he wanted to see her in the office. 'He didn't say anything else and he just kept walking towards his office. I wondered what it was he wanted to see me about, but it really didn't register with me what had happened or what I was about to hear. When I saw two policemen standing in the office I knew right away that something terrible had happened and I started to scream: "It's Johnny."'

Lila's supervisor took her straight from work to the hospital and, on the way kept saying to Lila: 'Pray, pray.'

'I have a great faith and firmly believe in the power of prayer, but that day I just couldn't pray. I know now that this was God's way of telling me that Johnny was gone and the prayers I would have prayed would have been of no use.'

On arrival at the hospital she was taken into an anteroom and a nurse came in to her. Lila asked if her husband had been injured and how bad the injuries were. The nurse replied by saying: 'There is no easy way of saying this, but your husband has died.'

The plans for his murder had begun the day before when a woman came to the timber merchants where John worked and ordered an amount of wood which she wanted delivered to an address in Olympic Drive in the Ballycoleman estate in Strabane. On the morning of the delivery, three gunmen from the IRA took over a house belonging to an elderly couple that lived there and held them hostage while they waited for their target to arrive.

Along with the driver of the delivery lorry, John did arrive and went to the front door of the house to tell the resident who had ordered the wood that her delivery had arrived. As he approached the door, the three killers began firing and John was hit three times in the chest and died before he reached the hospital. The driver of the lorry was also shot at but managed to make his escape uninjured.

John's body was brought back to his home that night for his funeral on the Saturday, when he was buried from the church where he and Lila had married those years before. In a fitting tribute, he was afforded full military honours as he was laid to rest. Just before his body left the house his youngest daughter wanted to say her goodbyes and, after a third attempt due to her grief, she finally stood beside her father's body and stroking his face said her tearful farewell to the father she loved and who loved her.

From the day he was murdered Lila refused to sleep in the bed they had shared and changed bedrooms. She even had the room redecorated in an attempt to overcome the grief and loss she was feeling but all to no avail. 'Every night afterward I thought that I could hear his cough or heard his car arriving at the house and after a year I sold the house and moved.'

With the courage of so many wives in similar situations, Lila had to live on for their children and see to their welfare. 'I had to learn to drive so that I could carry on taking them where they wanted to go the way it was with their father. It was the most stressful thing I ever had to do but I managed it and a year later I passed my driving test. I had to do it for the children.'

Except for his duties with the UDR, Lila and John spent all their spare time together and shared each other's interests, and living without him was very hard. 'I was immensely proud of him, scared for him, but glad that he was the type of person he was. John served 10 years in the UDR and was always advising his colleagues to be careful and looking after their welfare. He was a Lance Corporal and had passed the exam for his second stripe but never got it before he was murdered.'

Ten years after his murder, Lila's son introduced her to James, a widower, and after a first date their romance blossomed – they both found happiness again and eventually married.

Neil Joseph Patterson was jailed for fifteen years for his involvement in the murder with concurrent sentences for sixteen other terrorist offences. The sentences added up to one hundred and ninety nine years.

Tullyvallen Orange Hall Massacre
1 September 1975

Tullyvallen Orange Hall is situated on Altnamackin Road near Newtownhamilton in County Armagh. It is approximately one mile from the border with the Irish Republic and the usual meeting place for Guiding Star Temperance Orange Lodge.

On 1 September 1975 that particular group was holding one of its monthly meetings and, after opening proceedings with their obligatory prayers, were conducting their business when the doors burst open. It was 10.00 p.m. and two IRA gunmen had come into the hall and immediately began spraying everyone there with machine gun fire.

Members dived where they could to escape the bullets, but four men died that night, they were 80-year-old John Johnston, 70-year-old William McKee, 40-year-old James McKee, and 40-year-old Nevin McConnell.

Another man, William Herron, died two days later from his injuries and, while others were also injured, they thankfully survived.

One member, an off duty member of the security forces, had a gun with him that he was given for his personal protection; he fired back at the intruders and thought that he injured one of them. When he began firing the two fled but, when they reached the outside of the building, they fired again through the windows.

A twenty-two-year-old man from Cullyhanna was later convicted of the shooting and also the murders of Ulster Defence Regiment members, Joseph McCullagh and Robert McConnell. He was sentenced to seven life sentences, but was released under the terms of the Good Friday Agreement.

Gordon Wilson
122 February 1953 – 21 February 1983

"A happy, kindly, and smiling sergeant of the RUC, who was looking forward to celebrating his 30th birthday next day with his wife of only last summer and their little six-week-old baby girl, was brutally killed by terrorists as he awaited the patrol he was guarding while they purchased some food in a city carry-out." - Ulster Gazette and Armagh Standard.

Gordon Wilson was the firstborn in a family of four; he had two sisters, Florence and Sandra, and one brother, Sammy.

There was only eleven months between Gordon and Florence and, because of this slight age difference, the two were very close. Florence thinks of Gordon every day and has an abundance of happy memories of him, even from their early childhood days, spent around the family home in Warrenpoint, Co Down.

'Gordon was always my protector when we were children and, even at school, he looked out for me. One of my earliest memories is of Gordon and myself visiting with our next door neighbour, Mrs McCormack, lovingly known to us as "Cormick". She was a lovely lady and every time she went to town, Gordon and I used to sit on a wall near the house, sometimes for hours, waiting for her return. She always brought us liquorice, which was a real treat to us children in those days,' recalls Florence.

It was during their childhood that the children first became aware of the IRA, when they heard some adults talking about that organisation. While they didn't know what these three letters meant, in the coming years they were to find out the hard way.

Their father, William, was a disabled Japanese POW who suffered continuous ill health. The house in which the family lived did not have any electricity but, despite the lack of this basic amenity, the house was full of love and cheer and the children had a happy childhood playing in the countryside around their home.

Gordon showed signs of being quite an entrepreneur. As a young teenager he bred rabbits and guinea pigs, which he took to Newry on the school bus to sell to a local pet shop. This was a great attraction with the other children and they soon developed a love for any living creature themselves and often exchanged animals with each other. Gordon and his friends also had an interest in repairing pushbikes and this interest soon developed into repairs to scooters.

'All of his life he was a real teaser and joker - never nasty, always funny. He was a very jolly, happy-go-lucky person and, in later years, was very fond of his little nieces and nephews, whom he spoiled rotten. When he came to visit us, he always brought them chocolate and presents and used to throw his loose change into the air for them to catch,' said Florence.

On leaving school his first job was in Fishers hardware shop in Newry; he later became a bread man in Portadown and, even there, his caring nature showed through. One farmer rescued a fox cub and gave it to him. He looked after it until it was fully grown, but it was released back into the wild when it killed his mother's hens!

'At fifteen, Gordon became a Christian and along with one of his friends he used to organise missions at various halls around the Warrenpoint area. Gordon had preached his first sermon when he was only sixteen. As a committed Christian he often spoke of what the Lord had done in his life; it is only the comfort of knowing that Gordon is in heaven that helps our family to cope with his death. Daddy had died eight years previously and Mummy often says that she is only thankful the Lord took him away before Gordon's death, as he would never have survived the heartache of losing his eldest child at the hands of terrorism.'

Gordon joined the Ministry of Defence Police and was based at RAF Aldergrove, but he had always an ambition to serve in the RUC and joined up in 1974.

'Our parents pleaded with him not to join the RUC and Mum said to him that she would rather he didn't go, but it was what he wanted, and despite the fact that the terrorist campaign was then at its height, he went away for training. I remember the day he left home to start his training and we were all crying for fear of his life, as at the time there was a heavy death toll almost daily among the security forces. While we worried about him we knew this was what he wanted.'

After his training he was sent to Andersonstown in West Belfast and while there he was involved in two separate explosions, but escaped virtually uninjured. He sat and passed his Sergeants exam but, because he had only been in the Force for six months, he had to wait until he had served his probation before he could be given his promotion. On promotion he was transferred to Forkhill in South Armagh where he continued to experience the terrorist threat at close quarters.

In one particular incident some of his colleagues were ambushed in a police car. On another occasion the joint Police Station/Army Barracks was also attacked with mortar bombs. The lorry that had been used by the terrorists was needed by the police forensic team to collect any evidence as to who carried out the attack. It had already been checked for booby traps by the ATO and, after being cleared by them as safe, it was necessary to drive it to Gough Barracks, Armagh for examination. Someone had to be designated to drive the lorry and as Sergeant this decision was to be made by Gordon. A close friend of Gordon's was given the task, and when he started the engine, a bomb hidden in the windscreen washer bottle exploded, destroying the cab of the lorry. Gordon was very badly affected by this incident, as his colleague was badly injured in the explosion.

The family at home were always very anxious and almost dreading to listen to the news as nearly every day a member of the security forces was being murdered.

From Forkhill RUC Station, Gordon was transferred to Armagh City RUC Station, then on to the DMSU based at St Angelo in Enniskillen, and then back to H1 DMSU at Gough Barracks, Armagh. While serving in Enniskillen he met a lovely girl, Pat, who was to become his wife.

'Our mother often recalls how he told her that the day he met Pat, the sun started to shine in his life, (at the time he had been living with the constant threat on his and his colleagues lives), and had continued to shine ever since. The two of them were so happy together.'

When Pat and Gordon married, they set up home in Armagh; very soon they had a baby daughter, Kathy, and his happiness was now complete as, 'His child was everything to him'.

He used to bring his colleagues home to see little Kathy and, even when he was passing the house on duty, he would call in for a minute just to see her. One of these quick visits happened on the night of his death as he had just left his home from visiting with his wee family. He was really happy with his wife and child and he made no secret of it: 'they were his whole world'.

'My husband, George, and Gordon were best friends and whenever we were with Gordon and Pat he was always comparing Kathy's development to our baby son, David, who was three months older than her. He couldn't wait to see her first smile, her first steps, or to hear her call him Daddy – this never happened as Gordon was cruelly taken from us when Kathy was only six weeks old. With seeing him so often it helped give us reassurance, but our family still lived under a dreadful fear all of the time, especially when we heard of other members of the security forces being murdered.'

During 1982 the terrorist threat against security force families had become so serious that many people were forced to leave the homes they had lived in for all of their lives, and the Wilson family were no exception.

'There was a great threat on our family home at Warrenpoint and my brother Sammy (also an RUC officer) and mother were constantly being warned to move by the police. A few months before his death there was a lot of pressure put on Gordon by his superiors to have the family move and eventually they had to go. They were one of the last security force families to be put out of the area. This broke my mother's heart to have to leave her home, which always had an open door to all her friendly neighbours, both Protestant and Roman Catholic, and whom she misses to this day.'

Florence recalls one evening when she and her sister, Sandra, along with Gordon's wife Pat, all went for a walk together around the country lanes where the rest of her family had moved to. 'We were talking about one recent murder and the way the media had reacted at the time. We all agreed that there was an unnecessary intrusion into the families' grief and that they should have been allowed to mourn in peace. We never thought at the time that we would soon be in the same situation.'

For all the security personnel at the time the danger was constantly there, and for Gordon too, there was always the worry at the back of his mind.

On the Saturday night before he died he called his wife out of the kitchen into their living room where he was sitting nursing their baby. He wanted to tell Pat that he thought he would not live to see his 30th birthday and that the IRA would kill him. Naturally, Pat was very distraught to hear Gordon say such a terrible thing, but in a few short days his words were to come back to haunt her.

On Monday 21 February 1983, one day before his 30th birthday, Gordon was on mobile patrol in Armagh. At around eight o'clock in the evening one of the men in his patrol decided that he would like some fish and chips for his supper. They drove to Caffolas chip shop in Lower English Street. Whilst the Constable was purchasing his supper, Gordon got out of his armoured police car to provide cover and protection for him. Gordon and his other colleague took up separate positions on either side of the chip shop. Gordon was positioned a little way up the street outside a derelict building. Unknown to him, there was a bomb behind the door of the building he was positioned at. It was detonated by remote control from the grounds of the nearby St Patricks Roman Catholic Cathedral and Gordon died instantly in the explosion.

The bomb had been filled with six-inch nails and bolts and, at his inquest, it became known that forty of these had been imbedded in his body along with a wooden stake. He also suffered severe multiple injuries. The man who lived for his new family, and who had shown so much kindness and consideration to all he met in life, was no more.

Even on the day of Gordon's funeral, there was no escape from the hatred of those opposed to Her Majesty's Forces. The family remember the incident very vividly and were shocked at the hatred shown by Secondary School pupils whilst the funeral cortege was travelling through Canal Street in Newry. They were jeering, laughing, clapping, and giving the fingers towards the Union Jack draped coffin. It was the funeral of another policeman. They didn't even know him as a person, but their hatred still allowed them to gloat at the cowardly murder of a fellow human being. He was buried in Clonallon Churchyard in Warrenpoint after a service in the Presbyterian Church.

After Gordon's murder the family discovered that the Ulster Defence Regiment had been patrolling in the area earlier on the morning of the explosion and they had detected evidence of explosives in Lower English Street. They immediately put the area out of bounds and informed the authorities in Armagh Police Station and advised them to also put the area out of bounds to police personnel. However, the authorities dismissed the UDRs findings and the area was not placed out of bounds, a decision that subsequently cost Gordon his life.

The disclosure made the pain even worse for the family, knowing that if the RUC had acted on the information of the UDR, Gordon's life would have been spared. To this day the police have not told the family of any of the circumstances and they find this very hurtful.

His inquest was also carried out within eight weeks after his death while the family emotions were still very raw. To them this was very strange as other inquests took years to be heard. They have always wondered was this to cover up someone's negligence?

The North Armagh Brigade of the PIRA carried out the murder 22 years ago and Florence and her brother and sister still cannot find it in their hearts to forgive the people who did

Heather Kerrigan
20 May 1965 - 14 July 1984

Heather Kerrigan was always surrounded by friends and was, by nature, an outgoing and bubbly individual who loved life and lived it to the fullest.

When her sister Elma's husband was murdered she did everything possible to help alleviate the pain that she was feeling and bring back whatever semblance of normality she could to her.

'Heather was younger than me and, while I was the stay-at-home type, she was always out and about and involved with something or other. She was always right up-to-date with fashion and, whatever the fashion happened to be at a particular time, Heather had it. Growing up we had our differences but we were always close and, in fact, it was she who encouraged my romance with Thomas.'

On the night that they first met in the bar, Heather, who already knew Thomas, came across and began teasing him about 'chatting up her sister', but was pleased that the two seemed to like each other.

When they eventually married, Heather was a bridesmaid and Norman McKinley, a friend of Thomas, was best man to the couple.

'One other thing about Heather that was almost an obsession with her was her hair. She always had a comb with her and was forever combing her hair to make sure it was sitting properly. Even whenever she was dressed in the latest fashion, somewhere on her possession was her comb.'

Following Thomas's murder, Heather helped her sister in every way that she could, encouraging her to learn to drive and spending as much time with her as possible, and she and Elma became closer than ever.

'I remember one night when I was in my bed and she rang at two thirty in the morning to ask me to come to the top of the town to collect her. I had to drive there in my dressing gown and worried that I would be stopped at a military checkpoint or be seen by someone who knew me.'

Heather had also joined the Ulster Defence Regiment and, as a Greenfinch, did not carry arms but was there under the protection of her male colleagues to search female suspects on security patrol.

The bond between them grew and Heather spent many nights with her sister, and was with her the night before she went on her last patrol.

'She wasn't supposed to be on duty that morning, the 14 July 1984, but someone else had called in sick and she was asked to go. I remember her leaving and I said to her: "You remember you owe me £20, and she called to me that she hadn't forgotten."'

Elma was at her family home when someone called to say that there had been an explosion near the town and that some UDR personnel had been casualties.

As no one in the family had heard the explosion, or anything about it, another brother said that he would go to the army barracks and try to get any information he could about it.

While they waited, the family watched for his return and in the distance, on a road, which led to their house, they saw two cars coming towards them. As they drew nearer they waited and wondered until they came to a halt outside their door.

'One man got out, he was a former school teacher, he looked at us and simply shook his head. Then the local doctor and clergy arrived and that confirmed everything. Finally, another car drew up and my brother got out of it and he was crying and told us that Heather was dead, murdered.'

Heather had been on patrol on the outskirts of the town in one of two Land Rovers carrying UDR personnel and the IRA had planted a land mine at the side of one of the roads they would be using. As the patrol passed, the bomb was detonated from Corgorys Forest and the vehicle was blown off the road, the terrorists never faced their targets.

'Heather was killed instantly and so was Norman McKinlay who had been my best man. Heather had no injuries at all except for a slight cut on her foot, but Norman was very badly injured and had also died instantly,' said Elma. 'One thing that stands out from that time was when Norman's father called to the house that same day to express his sympathy. His own son had been murdered, but such was the measure of this man that he took the time to come to see us. I will never forget that and it shows how decent a human being he was.'

Heather was buried in the uniform she was so proud of, but she has left behind many memories of courage and care.

'She was very courageous to have joined and to have stayed on. She was only nineteen, but was brave beyond her years. I am very proud of her and always will be. I lost both a sister and a friend that day as well as my best man and friend. I miss her fun and everything about her and her memory is still with me. I miss so many things about her; I miss the times when she went shopping with me. There are still times when I hear people saying certain things that I think of her and even certain songs on the radio bring many memories flooding back.'

Following so many losses Elma found herself being over-protective towards her family and, on one occasion when her daughter wanted to go on a school trip, she found herself making all the excuses she could so that she could not go.

'It was only after the teacher spoke to me and gave me assurances that she would be well cared for that I allowed her to go. It is just one of the legacies that were left to me.'

No one has ever been caught for the murders of Thomas Loughlin, Heather Kerrigan, or Norman McKinley. They remain one of the many unsolved murders of members of the security forces and no public enquiries have ever been initiated by the Government.

Joseph James McIlwaine
29 July 1966 – 12 June 1987

When Joseph McIllwaine was born on 29 July 1966 he was the only boy in a family of six sisters who doted on their only brother. He was, literally, a blond-haired, blue-eyed boy who was the apple of his parent's eyes and, by all accounts, those of his sisters too. There were many willing baby sitters when they were needed and Joseph was given all the attention necessary.

As he grew, so did his identity and he developed a great love of horse riding and any type of outdoor pursuit, especially golf. Personality-wise, Joseph was a well-liked teenager and was a very willing individual, always there to help when he was asked.

'He never knew the meaning of the word "no" and would do anything to help anyone,' said his sister Janet Hunter. 'That was anything except feed the family dogs which, for some reason, he really didn't like. When he was asked he would always say: "In a minute", but the minutes went on and on. Sometimes one of us would do it for him, but most of the times we made him do it himself, as this was his responsibility,' she laughed. 'He was the sort of person who could win you around.'

Joseph left school at sixteen and found a job at Lisburn Golf Club and, in Janet's words, '... thought all of his dreams had come true, working on a golf course and getting paid for it.'

In their younger lives the family moved home a lot after the formation of the Ulster Defence Regiment as their father had joined soon afterwards.

'Because of what was happening in Northern Ireland he said that he could either be military or paramilitary, but as he had always been brought up to support the law, he would become military,' recalled Janet.

'For security we had to move a lot as our father's whereabouts became known. We even had to change the car a lot and our father even taught me how to check for bombs as I shared the family car with our father. It became a way of life for all the family just like the many moves we had to make. No one ever thought that the Troubles would last so long and, for as long as he was a member of the UDR, I worried about my father,' said Janet. 'I remember it came to the stage that when he was out on duty at night I couldn't sleep at all until I heard him come home and then I finally fell into a proper sleep.'

Like many families in Northern Ireland at the time there was always the constant worry for their loved ones who were patrolling the countryside or towns and villages in the fight against terrorism, many giving their lives by doing so.

'Not sleeping became routine for me during dad's time in the UDR, I was always uneasy until he came home. Then I could relax, we were all together again and nothing bad had happened to us at home or to dad while he was on duty. Even with all that we feared we still all supported what dad was doing and the reasons he was in it.'

Her father stayed in the Regiment for eight years until he had to retire due to illness and it was only then that Janet began to sleep properly.

As the years passed, Joseph and his family grew up and eventually each of them found partners and began making their own lives in the world. Joseph met a girl who was to become his fiancée. Janet got married and made her own home away from the family house.

The Troubles continued and the family still were careful about their security, a legacy from the many threats they had received over the years.

'I remember one day I went to see Joseph and his fiancée where they were living and I can't remember what it was I wanted but, when he opened the boot of his car, I saw a camouflage uniform inside it. I immediately asked him what it was and what he was doing with it. He told me that he had joined the Ulster Defence Regiment about six months previously. It was probably because he knew we would worry that he hadn't told us as that was the sort of person he was, genuinely good. I did worry again after that but he assured us that he would be alright.'

Janet recalled a time when Joseph was eighteen months old and she was playing along with him on the outside steps of the house that they had recently moved to.

'I was swinging on the rails of the steps and Joseph tried to do it too, but fell over and received quite a severe bump to his head. That fall should have done more damage as it really was severe but he was fine in a few minutes and I suppose from that time on I thought that he was indestructible,' she said.

On the morning of 12 June 1987, Janet was going to Belfast with some friends and, for some reason, left a phone number with her in-laws to say where she could be reached if she was needed. 'I had never done that before and I still don't know what made me do it that particular day, it must have been providential.'

She had just reached her destination when her mother called her and said: 'Come home, Joseph has been shot.' 'I asked, was he dead' but she just said again for me to come home, which I did.

Joseph had been at work that day doing the job he loved and as usual went with three colleagues at 10.00 a.m. to have his mid-morning break. They went there at the same time every day and their 'canteen' was a garage storeroom with only one door as an entrance and exit and no windows. Just after they had arrived the door was flung open and a number of gunmen stood at the entrance. They asked for the ACE men at gunpoint and instantly shot Joseph twelve times.

'He was hit once in the head and the other bullets hit him on the chest and abdomen. He had no chance of escape and he died immediately.'

By the time Janet reached her parents home, other members of the family had already arrived as the news had reached them in various ways. 'Two friends of ours were at the UDR base when the news came in and it was they who told my parents what had happened. One of my sisters was in town and sitting in her car when she heard it on the radio and she rushed home. It was only after we had all gathered that the police arrived to tell us that Joseph had been murdered.'

None of the family was allowed to go to Joseph as the police forensics worked in the area of the shooting. 'That was hard to take and his body lay there until 7.00 that night. It got to the stage that my father even asked the police to put a blanket over him because he was "getting cold".'

On the day of his funeral Joseph was buried with full military honours, a lone piper played a lament, and was given the recognition that he deserved for his service. 'He had no chance of escape or opportunity to defend himself and was a very easy target for the cowards who murdered him.'

The IRA claimed the murder and, even on the day of his funeral, the family did not have the opportunity to grieve in peace. 'Someone rang the house and said that they knew where all the family lived and where the children went to school and that they would do the same again.'

Janet claims that Joseph knew he was in danger, but still was intent on doing what he felt was his duty by serving his country. 'He told me one time that he was threatened at a checkpoint and another time when he was working on the golf course. Because of this he had applied to the police for a personal weapon for his protection and a family friend of ours went with him when he made the application. It never arrived, since then it was told that there was no record of his request in the police station yet we know that he was there. This is still a contention with Joseph's parents, would it have been different if Joseph had have been able to protect and defend himself.'

Six years ago Janet formed a victim support group in Lisburn Families Achieving Change Together (FACT), and offers a support and counselling service to the all too many who need that help. 'I started with my own family, one of my sisters who had been in hospital with the threat of premature birth of her third baby, when Joseph was shot and was not able to even attend his funeral; she left and went to live in the UK. We traced her and reunited the family and I believe that with all the families who have suffered through terrorism we can bring about a change.'

When asked if she forgave her brother's killers, Janet had no hesitation in saying: 'I have no feeling whatever for them, I would want them to pay for what they did and go to prison. I know that the person who drove the car that day is still walking around Lisburn and I would love to see that person brought to justice.'

As an evangelical Christian she said that she has no doubt that she will be with Joseph again one day, but until then she misses him, misses having him around and seeing his smile.

Kenneth Lynch
16 May 1955 – 2 June 1977

Ken Lynch was born on 16 May 1955, the third son of Anna and William Lynch from the little Tyrone village of Donemana, with a younger sister completing the family of four. Like most young boys his age, his life included an abiding love of football and, in particular, his favourite team, Manchester United.

During his school years, while he succeeded well in his education, nothing surpassed his enthusiasm for the sport and, when he could, he was to be found playing his favourite game as his mother Anna recalls.

'Ken was the tallest and broadest of my sons and loved to play football whenever and wherever he could as it took priority over everything else in his life. The only thing that came close to it was his appetite and he certainly loved his food, but I suppose he needed to eat to keep up his energy levels. He was like many of his friends, eating and running back outside to play another game, and getting into the usual fisticuffs over various disagreements. Even when he was older he used to travel to see Manchester United playing, but he never told me where he was until he came home as he knew that I would have worried about him going on a boat to England.'

With some encouragement Ken would also be of assistance around the family home or in the shop, which his parents had at the time, and in his mother's words was '… very helpful when he could be tied down; he was a very good-natured child. He was very caring towards people, and to his father and I in particular, all of my children were and Ken carried that care with him right through his life.'

As he grew older the murder campaign by terrorists was already leading the news headlines in Northern Ireland, but Ken began to express an interest in joining the Royal Ulster Constabulary, much to the concern of his mother.

'He was working in DuPont outside Londonderry at the time, but wanted to be a policeman and he had been talking about this from his teenage years,' recalled his mother. 'When he first mentioned it I was really worried and said to him about the number of policemen who were being killed, but he still wanted to join up. There was nothing I could say to change his mind so he first of all joined the RUC Reserve. I was worried but he was doing what he wanted to do and when I said to him about the possibility of being shot he used to say: "As long as they take me right and I am not left maimed". Ken was always active and he couldn't have accepted being an invalid, but what he said didn't do anything to take my worries away.'

After a term in the Reserves he wanted to join fulltime and, after making application and following the usual interviews and examinations, he was eventually accepted.

'Being six-foot-two in height and a strong build and having been in the Reserves, I suppose it was inevitable he would be accepted, but on the night that he told me, I was really worried about it. I didn't say anything, as I didn't want to spoil his delight at getting his ambition. I just kept my thoughts to myself as I couldn't have changed his mind anyway.'

Following his training, Ken was stationed in Cookstown in Co Tyrone and soon fell into the routine of duties and patrols around the area. On his days off he went back to the family home to stay and, in his many regular phone calls home, he would tell of his impending visits and always had one special request for his mother.

'He always said that I was to have a lemon meringue pie made for him as he liked them and I suppose it was part of his home life and I always had one for him,' said Anna. 'I haven't made any since he died as I just can't bring myself to make one, and there are so many other things I miss.'

On the weekend of 28 May 1977 Ken came home to spend time with his family and to catch up with some of his friends. It was an ordinary weekend and he had his favourite pie as usual and nothing was amiss with the family. On the Sunday morning he went with his family to morning service, as this was Children's Day within the Presbyterian Church. He travelled with his father and one of his brothers and there was nothing at all out of the ordinary about the day, except it was to be the last time that any of them would see him alive.

'That night I went back to the evening service and, when I was driving home, I saw Ken in his car driving towards me. We both stopped and he said that he was heading back to Cookstown, but that he would phone me through the week, probably on Thursday. Then he said goodbye and drove off,' recalled Anna. 'I never thought at the time that this would be our last conversation and I drove on home.'

The following Thursday the policemen in Cookstown were asked for three volunteers to go to Stewartstown to help man the station there as some of their colleagues there had to make court appearances and the area would have been short of the necessary quota for full protection.

Along with Reserve Constable Hugh Henry Martin and Constable Derek Davidson, Ken volunteered for the task and the three of them set off for their temporary posting. Ken was a front seat passenger and, as they passed through Ardboe at 2.40 p.m. enroute to their destination, an IRA gang who had lain in wait for a police target ambushed them.

Hugh Martin and Ken were killed instantly, but Derek Davidson was still alive when the ambulance and other police arrived. He helped carry his two dead colleagues into an ambulance and, when he was himself being taken to hospital, he too died. Unknown to Derek, he was suffering from internal bleeding and half-an-hour after the ambush and like all of his murdered colleagues, he had shown tremendous courage and concern for his fellow man right up to the end.

While this was happening, Anna was helping some members of her family clear out a house that had been vacated by another family member. 'At twenty past four the phone in the house rang and, when I answered it, I heard my husband asking me to come back home as quickly as I could. I asked him if something had happened Ken, but he just said to come home. Inside me I knew that something had happened to my son and, when I reached the house, I saw the car of our family doctor on the road and I knew then for definite that something terrible had happened to him.'

When she was told of the day's events, Anna admits that she was devastated and unable to deal with the fact that her youngest son had been assassinated by a gang of terrorists who knew nothing about him, but had set out that day to do murder. 'It was my husband and one of my sons who had to go and identify his body at the South Tyrone Hospital in Dungannon; a lot of friends went with them to accompany the cortege back home. I couldn't go as I was so upset, but I waited on him to come back home again.'

Many friends called at the family home over the next few days – the numbers were a testimony to the popularity of the young man and to his family. 'One police woman stayed the whole time so that she could help us in whatever way possible and I have to say that her kindness and assistance was invaluable at a time when we needed it most.'

On the day of Ken's funeral he was buried with full police honours, his coffin was draped with the Union flag and the police band led the procession from his home to the family church for his service.

'I went to the service and was coping well until his coffin was lifted up to be carried out of the church. That was just too much for me and I think that I collapsed. I had to be taken home and put to bed and that is about all I remember for a while. I couldn't even come back downstairs when everyone came back for something to eat after the funeral service.'

Even today, so many years after the loss of her son, Anna still has many difficulties in dealing with his murder. 'I still miss his smile and the telephone calls to say when he was coming home and to have his lemon meringue pie ready for him. I have not baked one since. I miss his company and I miss so many things about him. If I had the time over again with him I would still worry about him joining the police but I know that it would have made no difference to him. He was only in the fulltime police for ten months before he was murdered and I know that had he survived he would have made it his career and would have moved up the ranks. There is not a night in life that I don't think about him and I don't need anniversaries or birthdays to remind me of him, he is with me all the time. I know where he is now, but I can't say the same for his killers. I would rather be Ken than the people who murdered him.'

Robert (Bobby) Stott
6 November 1954 – 25 November 1975

Bobby Stott was a friend to everyone he met and everyone he met was his friend, except for those who shot him in the back and stomped on his face as he lay dying.

He was born the fifth child of a family of nine children, four boys and five girls, in the gate lodge of Riverview Park in Londonderry on 6 November 1954. The house they shared with their parents was small, very small for the number of occupants it held, but it came along with the job his father held as caretaker of some local government offices.

Like many other Protestant families at the time, the Stotts were not included among the privileged classes but had to work hard for anything they had and, like those other families, it was not a lot.

His sister Margaret recalls those days which, although hard, were happy times as no one knew any better, but simply struggled through on a day to day basis. 'Looking back, the times were indeed hard and there was not a lot of money to keep the family through the week and certainly not any for squandering or for treats. We made it through each week with a struggle, but we had each other and we were happy with that. Those were days when the community helped each other and everyone knew each other's circumstance. I can remember one local bakery being over generous with bread and other fancy breads whenever we went in to buy something from them. That was the sort of help that was common in those days and which certainly helped us through many lean times.'

Church sales were another focal point – an important event for many families from the Protestant tradition; many children were clothed from articles they came across at these fundraisers.

When he was only ten years old Bobby's mother died and, along with the heartache, the family's situation became even more difficult.

'Our mother worked as a cleaner in the offices where our father was caretaker and her wages were also vital for our keep and keeping food on the table,' explained Margaret. Our eldest brother suffered from rheumatoid arthritis and was unable to work and, with so many children in the family, life was already difficult and looked as though it was going to get worse.'

The final solution was that Margaret herself would leave school and take over the mother's role as cleaner and caretaker to the rest of the family and, at fifteen years of age, she became an adult and took on all the responsibilities of her new position.

Bobby was attending Carlisle Road Primary School when his mother died and, like all of his brothers and sisters, he too was badly affected by her death, a loss that was to stay with him until he too left this life to be with her.

After Primary School he moved to Templemore Intermediate School where he made lots of new friends and became a popular pupil who did well in his education.

In his teenage years the family moved to an apartment in Londonderry's Guildhall where his father had obtained the position of caretaker and, for the first time in their lives, they had a bathroom, central heating, and more space to live than they ever had before. Compared to what they had just left, this was total luxury and they began to enjoy their new environment with all the amenities, but this didn't last long.

A few years after their move the IRA planted a bomb inside the building and their apartment, along with offices and the Council Chamber, were blown up. One of those responsible for planting the bomb went on to become Mayor of the city many years later.

From there Bobby and his family moved to Fountain Street and lived in the residential part of a former public house and again took a retrograde step as far as accommodation was concerned as here there was no central heating and the facilities were quite basic. However, the family accepted their circumstance and, with each other for support, made the best of the situation.

'I remember we each had our own jobs to do in the house and Bobby's was to wash the backyard and step every day or polish the linoleum, and he did this without complaint on most occasions. He was very helpful and was always concerned for the rest of us.'

Fountain Street was, and still is, a loyalist enclave on the West Bank of the city and an area not known for being affluent but one which, although filled with decent, hard working people was still one of the poorer areas of the city and which, in today's definitions, would have been described as a Protestant ghetto.

No one in the area had more than basic amenities and very few had a bathroom or hot running water. Many families had to squeeze into a two up, two down terrace house and, in more than a few instances, had extended family sharing the house.

Having been born on this side of the River Foyle the family, and Bobby in particular, preferred to accept their new abode rather than move to the Waterside where they could have had a better type of home.

As a person Bobby was a quiet individual, always a diplomat, someone who fought a constant battle with his weight. Among his many friends he was known as 'the fat man', not so much as an insult but as a term of endearment as he had many of the qualities normally associated with those people deemed overweight. Bobby was jolly and always had a ready smile for his friends and for any stranger he met.

'He was the peace maker in any troubled situation and was always a sucker for a sad story, often doing everything he could to alleviate any problem he heard about,' recalled Margaret. 'Above all else, Bobby was a Unionist and a staunch Presbyterian. He was a long term member of the Young Unionist movement but received no special privileges for doing so, we still lived from hand to mouth in a house that by today's standards would have been condemned.'

As soon as he could he left school and got a job in a local shirt factory doing all sorts of jobs from cutting shirts to keeping the girls supplied with materials. 'Every week he handed his full wage packet into the house to help feed the rest of the family and, in particular, those coming after him.'

In the 1960s the Northern Ireland Civil Rights Association began holding marches in Northern Ireland seeking 'civil rights for Catholics' and in Londonderry the Derry Housing Action Committee held a number of protests to highlight the plight of Roman Catholics whom they claimed were living in bad housing conditions.

No approaches were ever made to the people of The Fountain to ask them about their appalling housing conditions or for them to join any protests or marches appealing for better housing conditions. Instead, they were promoted as the privileged section of the community who had it all as opposed to the rest who were persecuted and deprived by the British community.

While the Civil Rights Movement paraded through the City on 5 October 1968 demanding better conditions for one section of the community, the Protestant families in The Fountain still had to make do with outside toilets, overcrowding, damp houses, and no running hot water.

During the months following the march, The Fountain was attacked and petrol bombed on a regular basis by those who thought that the working class, impoverished residents of the area were responsible for their conditions.

Through it all Bobby and many like him continued to work for their living and never demanded, as much as they would have liked it, for any handouts by the government. Their ethos was that they should work for anything they needed and that, when it was possible and funds were available, their lot in life would be improved.

Some years after their move to The Fountain, that situation did arise and a redevelopment programme was announced for the area and after years of making do with living in half a house, the bar section of their home was unusable, the family were allocated a new house in the area. This was a major improvement, but still the financial hardship remained with them and still they carried on with no privileges whatsoever and continued to work for their living which, although improved by accommodation, was not one of affluence.

As his wages improved Bobby was able, for the first time in his life, to buy a new suit of which he was justifiably proud and, whenever the occasion arose, when it could be worn, Bobby wore it with pride.

It was around the same time that the Ulster Defence Regiment came into existence and, along with other members of his family, he joined up.

'It was not for the money, nor to suppress the Roman Catholic population, but as a form of service to our country and Bobby was proud of his country and his allegiance. As our father was ex-service himself, I suppose it was the most natural thing for us to do and follow his example.'

The extra money was a help to both him and the family, who by this time had met their future partners, got married, and were moving from the family home, but still Bobby wanted to remain in the area in which he was born and where he had grown up.

All of his life he still missed the mother he had loved and talked about her often to his friends – staying in the vicinity he knew was for him a link with that part of his life that he still longed for. He still continued to work at the factory where he had made many friends among his colleagues of both religions and still remained an active member of the Young Unionists.

There were times, particularly after yet another murder of a colleague in the UDR, the family would touch on the possibility of one of them being attacked. 'He used to say to us that if we were ever in a situation where the IRA tried to kidnap us that we were to run as they would kill us anyway and that we shouldn't allow ourselves to be taken easily.'

That was not the way it happened for Bobby, his killers couldn't face him, but lay in ambush to murder him. A week before he died the girls in the factory where he worked had bought him a cigarette lighter and within days Bobby had lost it. He questioned every member of the family as to its whereabouts, but it could not be found and he was devastated by its loss.

On Tuesday 25 November 1975 he left his work and walked through a drizzle to go home and get ready for plans he had made for that night. It was less than half a mile to his house and, to get to it, he had to walk through one of the gateways in the famous city walls to get into the estate. It was dark and, at that time of the evening, most people were already home and having their evening meal and that, along with the drizzle, kept most people off the street.

Bobby walked as he always did, with his hands in the pockets of whatever coat he was wearing and his head slightly bent and looking at the ground. He would have been in a hurry to get indoors and would not have been paying particular attention to what was going on around him.

He reached The Fountain and walked along the path that led to his new home, passing the other houses in the terraced row where he lived. Just when he reached the steps that led to his door, at least two gunmen came out of the shadows and shot him ten times in the back, he fell just feet from security.

After they had shot him, one of them stomped on the side of his face before they made off into the shadows from where they had come. It was while he lay dying on the street that his eldest brother found him, but because of his disability, he couldn't lift his younger brother off the ground. Bobby was taken to Altnagelvin Hospital where he died from his wounds with many friends and family around him.

'I remember when we were leaving the house on the day of his funeral our father called us all together and said to us: "Hold your heads up high when we walk out and don't let them see that they have hurt us." I would rather have a son who was murdered than have a son who is a murderer,' said Margaret.

He was buried with full military honours following a service in his beloved First Derry Presbyterian Church and, some months later, the Young Unionists presented a lectern to the church in his memory. 'Some years later when we were looking through a box which contained mementos of our mother we came across Bobby's cigarette lighter, so he must have been looking in it himself a few days before he died and dropped the lighter into it himself,' said Margaret.

Richard Latimer
6 February 1942 – 7 June 1980

County Fermanagh in Northern Ireland is arguably the most beautiful of all the counties in the Province with its lakes, picturesque small towns and villages, and rolling countryside. It is also where many murders of members of the security forces and other innocents took place.

Bonnie Latimer was just sixteen and a half when she met the man with whom she fell deeply in love and who was to become her husband a few years after their first meeting.

'I was working in a children's home in Larne when I came back to my home in Newtownbutler for a short holiday. There was a dance in the town that night and as I love dancing I went along and it was there that I met Richard. We had a few dances and talked a lot that night and, at the end of the evening, he asked to walk me home and I readily accepted,' she explained.

Unfortunately, her time at home was almost up and she had to return to her work but, after a few months, she decided to return to her hometown again for good.

'I would have to be honest and say that it was because of Richard that I came back and it was soon after that when I saw him again and I suppose that was when our romance began. He was good looking, kind, and generous, and was everything any girl could want. We continued going out for a few years and then we got married.'

When she was twenty years old Bonnie and Ritchie, as she called him, got engaged and a year later got married in Gallon Parish Church in Newtownbutler.

A year after their wedding they were blessed with their first child, and three years after that they had their second and the family was complete.

Ritchie managed a shop in the town and was always a great provider for his wife and children; he and Bonnie still kept up with their dancing and, while her parents looked after their children on a Saturday night, the two always went to follow their pastime.

'He eventually bought the shop and we had many happy times during our years together and he always made sure the family were well provided for. We had a comfortable life and had holidays every year, usually to Blackpool or somewhere in Scotland.'

In 1979 the whole family made their first trip abroad when they went on holiday to Majorca and enjoyed it so much that Bonnie said to her husband that they should arrange to go again the following year. 'I have always remembered what he said when I made the suggestion, he said that we would not make any decisions, just take a day at a time.'

Like many others Ritchie had joined the Ulster Defence Regiment when it was formed in 1970 to counteract the threat and murder campaign from terrorists and the family were soon to see at firsthand the destruction and mayhem caused by them.

'The first incident was when a bomb was left in the doorway of the shop and, when it exploded, it caused minor damage to the front. We carried on trading as usual, but the second bomb was worse.'

The second bomb was not so minor, but consisted of one thousand pounds of explosive packed inside a car that was left outside their shop. It exploded and totally destroyed the building, along with others beside it; and, along with their business, their home above it was also destroyed. 'We had to live in a caravan for eighteen months until everything was built again and then we moved back.'

Unknown to Bonnie, there was a major threat on Ritchie's life and he had been receiving police protection to and from his work. 'There were also Ulster Defence Regiment members sitting in the shop as protection and I didn't know.'

Even without knowing the seriousness of her husband's situation, Bonnie worried about him every time he went out on duty. 'He used to say to me that there was no need to worry as he would do whatever worrying was necessary, but I still did.'

She recalls the nights when the children were asleep and he was out patrolling the countryside with his colleagues. 'I would sit at the bedroom window and watch for him to come home. When I saw his car arriving home I would hurry into bed and pretend to be asleep so that he wouldn't know that I had stayed up waiting for him. I didn't want to add to whatever worries he might have had. I think that every UDR wife in the country did the same, worried and kept watch.'

On the morning of Saturday 7 June 1980 the family woke as usual and, after having breakfast, they each went their own way. 'There was a Festival in Lisnaskea town that day and the children had wanted to go. Initially, I didn't want to go, but Ritchie said that the children wanted to and that while I was there he needed me to collect some wallpaper from one of the shops that he needed for a customer in ours.'

Bonnie took the children and, after watching the Festival, they all went back to the car and drove to collect the wallpaper.

Earlier in the day she had seen some Army vehicles rushing through the town and, from general experience in Northern Ireland, such a scene could only mean one thing.

'I said to the girl in the shop where I had gone to collect the wallpaper, God help whatever family those are for, someone's been shot.'

After making the comment, she went around the back of the shop to a storeroom to collect her errand and, on her return, the assistant was just coming off the telephone and was crying. 'I asked her what was wrong and she just said that everything was fine so I didn't want to push the matter and I left the shop.'

After leaving, Bonnie drove on to Newtownbutler and home and, on arrival at the outskirts of the town, she came on a UDR checkpoint. 'When the soldiers manning it saw me they waved me through, I thought that was very strange but I carried on and drove to my mother's house to drop off some items that I had bought for her.'

A cousin of Ritchie lived next door to her mother and, when she saw Bonnie, she called her into the house. At the same time two other friends approached the house and Bonnie said that she knew immediately that something had happened to her husband.

'I asked if he had been injured and, when I didn't get an answer, I knew than that he was dead.' Ritchie was indeed dead and had been shot by an IRA gunman who came into the shop and killed him.

'In a well planned operation the terrorists had waited until the UDR guards had left the shop and the police had taken up security outside. They arranged for a car to be set alight at the top of the town to draw the police away to investigate and, when they did, the gunman went inside.'

There were three customers outside when the gunman entered and, as Ritchie was with one at the back of the shop, he could not get a clear shot so he waited. Eventually his accomplice who was in a car outside came in and shouted to him: 'What's keeping you?'

The gunman then fired one shot at Ritchie that hit him in the back. As he ran outside, he tripped and, in his panic, released another shot that stuck in the frame of the door. 'When she heard the shot, the lady from the shop next door ran to help Ritchie and she cradled him in her arms as he died. I will be forever grateful for that and I am relieved that there was at least a friend with him as he died.'

Ritchie was taken to the Erne Hospital but was pronounced dead on arrival, and his body was brought back home the following day. He was buried from the church where he and Bonnie married with full military honours but, at her request, there was no gun salute. 'I couldn't have listened to the noise of a gun going off, but I did want every honour given to Ritchie as possible.'

A few days after the funeral, the family doctor, who was also a friend, took Bonnie and one of her children to visit the shop and see where her beloved Ritchie had died. 'I found it hard to go inside and the only way I can describe it was as if there was an iceberg at the door and I had to push against it to get inside. When I did get in and saw where it had happened I felt ice cold.'

From the shop they went to Ritchie's grave and, on the way back to the car, Bonnie took a severe panic attack. 'I was rushed home and had to be wrapped in blankets and given a few spoonfuls of brandy as, apparently, my heart had stopped and my eyes had rolled back into my head as I was very near death myself,' she said.

Recalling the day she came home after hearing that her beloved husband was dead, she said that when she realised that he had washed the dishes they had used that morning before he went to his work, it almost broke her heart.

'For a long time afterwards I always set the table for four people as I couldn't accept that he was gone and it was only for our children's sake that I was able to carry on. I kept the shop for four years after he died, but then I sold it as there were too many memories. Words can't describe what I feel for those people who murdered him, but I do know that he was a better man than any of them, he thought a lot of his country and, despite the threat of the terrorists, he did what he did with courage and he had a lot of courage,' she said.

Of Ritchie himself, she said: 'We were very much in love, we never went anywhere without each other and we as a family always had his love and support. I miss his presence, his conversations, and most of all I miss him. He was a wonderful man and an even better human being.'

Darkley Massacre

20 November 1983

It was the evening of Sunday 20 November 1983. The congregation of Mountain Lodge Pentecostal Church gathered as usual for their Sunday act of worship just outside the village of Darkley in County Armagh.

Two of the church elders, 59-year-old Harold Brown and 39-year-old Victor Cunningham were in the porch to welcome any late arrivals, and 44-year-old David Wilson was further inside the church.

The congregation had just sung the opening hymn, Are You Washed In The Blood Of The Lamb, when their worship was interrupted by gunfire as the building came under attack by a group who called themselves the South Armagh Republican Action Group.

They had already shot and killed Harold Brown and Victor Cunningham in cold blood, and then fired at David Wilson who was hit in the stomach. He bravely made his way into the church to call to the congregation to take cover as the gunmen stepped over the bodies of those they had killed and came inside the church itself to shoot at the congregation.

As they dived to take cover, the gunmen fired indiscriminately – seven of the worshippers were injured.

When their magazines were empty, they went back outside, reloaded, and fired again through the walls of the building, before making their escape.

David Wilson died in a small room at the back of the church from the injuries that he received.

Kenneth Graham
10 November 1943 – 27 April 1990

Throughout their bloody campaign of bombing and murder, the terrorists of Northern Ireland did not discriminate in who their victims would be but, while most of their outrages were against the security forces and property. They also targeted others because of their religion or their profession.

All across the Province, individuals were murdered because of their involvement in business or industry, with no other logic behind their killings other than the fact that they were helping the economy of the country or area where they lived. On 2 February 1977 industrialist Jeff Agate was murdered at his Talbot Park home in Londonderry by the IRA. On 2 December 1975 Lexie Mitchell and Charlie McNaul, who worked for a timber merchants, also in Londonderry, were gunned down while sitting in The Leprehaun café on Strand Road.

Similar murders occurred all over Northern Ireland with no reason, or a flimsy reason given by the terrorists, for having carried them out. In every case the family of those killed had to carry on in life with the horror of knowing that they would never see their loved one again and, for all of them, the grief brought about great turmoil in their lives.

Kenneth Graham was born on 10 November 1943, the third in a family of thirteen children. With his eight brothers and four sisters he lived in Kilkeel in County Down where his father was a building contractor and, in the ensuing years, it was because he became involved in the family business that he too was to become a target for the men of violence.

As a person Kenneth was 'obliging and kind', according to one of his sister's, Pam, who recalls that life with the brother, who was the kingpin of the business, was great fun. 'Our mother said that as a baby he was one of those children who slept all day and cried all night, but as he grew older and the rest of the family came along, he was great fun as a brother.'

At school Kenny was a moderate student and, on leaving, instead of taking up an automatic position in the family firm, he was sent to learn his trade in another builder retailers.

'He was great fun as a brother and his laughter could always be heard wherever he was; even coming into a room the first sign of his approach was his laugh,' recalled Pam. 'When all of my brothers got together it was fun to listen to them all talk and laugh at the practical jokes they had played during their working day.'

When he eventually joined the family firm Kenny stayed in the office to run that side of the business for his father; his obliging personality was one of his most endearing qualities.

He had his mischievous side too and Pam remembers the time before he married and when he stayed out later than permitted and could have been in trouble at home had he been caught. 'He used to climb up the drainpipe rather than come through the door and that way he was never caught. He gave one hundred and ten per cent to everything he did in life.'

Eventually Kenny married and left the family home but still called every day to keep his father informed of everything that was happening in the business. Unfortunately his marriage didn't last, but with his work and being the father of two children whom he loved, life carried on for him and he still called at his parent's home every morning as usual to spend time with all of the rest of his family. 'They all gathered at ten o'clock and it was still fun listening to them and hearing about their life, it was part of the daily routine for our parents.'

Being in the construction business the family took on whatever work was available and one job was the dismantling of a building in nearby Bessbrook, and some security work connected with it. To the family it was just another job but, to the terrorist, it was an excuse to take another innocent life, and they did so without mercy and in the most cowardly of ways.

On 26 March 1990 Kenny had been working with some branches and a piece of wood had somehow got into his eye. It was irritating quite badly and he decided to make the journey to Belfast to the Accident and Emergency Department of the Royal Victoria Hospital to have it treated.

As was usual, Kenny had parked his car on the driveway of his house and he had made arrangements with a friend to drive him there. Part of the arrangements was that he would drive himself to the friend's house and then leave from there. The driveway from his home was on a slope and, as he drove down towards the road, the car exploded with Kenny inside and taking the main blast of the explosion. The bomb had been placed under the driver's seat and was triggered by the movement of the car so that there was no chance whatever of escape.

A nurse lived directly opposite the house but, despite her best efforts and that of a relative who also arrived on the scene, there was nothing anyone could do.

Just a year previously, another brother had been killed outside Kenny's house in a traffic accident and now another member of the family had had their life taken from them, this time, not by accident, but by a calculated murder.

In her home Pam was totally unaware of what had happened until a neighbour came to call with her. 'She asked me if what she had heard was true and, when I invited her inside, all I can remember hearing was the words Kenneth and bomb,' said Pam. 'The information she had was that there had been a bomb under the driver's seat and that he had been very seriously injured.'

Kenny had died from his injuries and, like his brother before him, was buried from Kilkeel Presbyterian Church, where a large number of mourners came to pay their last respects. Like so many before them, the family were left with many questions, but with no answers about their brother's murder.

'I always had a gut feeling that he had been worried or concerned about something, but he never said that anything was bothering him. I wondered if he had been receiving threatening calls or something like that. I wondered if those who killed him had carried out dummy runs before they planted the bomb, had they been given information about his movements, or had they sat and watched while it exploded.'

Pam even began to question her faith and blamed God for what had happened, particularly after having lost another brother a year earlier. 'Our father died a year after that and I feel that his death was in some way due to what happened Kenny,' she said. 'I struggled greatly with my feelings after that, I knew as a Christian that I should forgive but, being honest, in my heart I knew that I could never forgive those who did this. They had left two children without a father, and parents without a son, and the rest of us without a brother.'

Eventually Pam stopped going to church, something which had played a large part in her life, as she said that she was 'so angry' with God for what had happened. 'I then found that whenever there was a crisis I was praying to God for help and, because I was, I decided to go back to church and, although it took a while, my faith has now returned and I feel more at peace.'

While the family has come to accept what has happened, there is not a day at the ten o'clock table when Kenny's name is not mentioned or at other times throughout the day.

That's as it should be.

William John Clarke
12 June 1921 – 3 August 1980

The people of Northern Ireland are well known for their ability for hard work and, in the majority of cases, for their attitude that, where possible, you earned your keep and were primarily responsible for providing for the needs of your family. In times of difficulty these people tightened their resolve and, despite many hardships, they carried on in time-worn fashion to do what was best for those they loved and for their country, often at great cost.

William Clarke was such a man, one who worked hard all his life and provided for his wife Elizabeth, their three sons and one daughter.

'In his younger years he worked in the Nestles factory in Victoria Bridge making chocolate and, after finishing his day's work, he would then go and work for some of the local farmers,' recalled one of his sons, Norman. 'He loved farming and he leased some land where he kept some pigs and cattle and grew vegetables, and I remember when we were all younger going out to work with him in the fields. We cut and piled turf from the bog and I remember driving the tractor and baler or gathering potatoes. We had a great time working with him out in the fields. He was a man who just kept going and was never sick and was, above all, a great father.'

Norman recalled the days, which seemed so far away from those of the present, when he and others in the family would help their father to harvest the cereal crops and bale the hay during the summer days in preparation for the coming winter. 'They were good days with many happy memories and the effort was all for us, his family, so that we would be well cared for and have everything we needed. He was a great provider for us, very fair but quite strict. Every Christmas and birthday there would be presents for all of us and while we were never spoiled we were certainly never neglected by him.'

In the earlier years of the terrorist threat, William had joined the B Specials to help patrol the borders and guard key installations to prevent easy movement for the would-be killers and bombers.

Like many men at the time, after a full day's work, he spent long hours on patrol in an attempt to protect the county and its people from threat and danger.

When the Ulster Defence Regiment was formed in 1970 to replace the Specials, William enlisted along with his son Norman and the two began their duties of patrolling and guarding in the new regiment.

'We spent a lot of the time guarding the police station in Castlederg and I think that in the time we spent working together we became very close,' said Norman.

Just as it was across the country, no one knew where the next attack would come from, and the men and women who gave up their free time and all too often their lives carried on with their job in the most dangerous era the British Isles had ever known.

In Norman's case, one of his first encounters with terrorism up close was when his patrol was called to an explosion. 'The explosion was caused by a bomb going off prematurely and the two terrorists who were carrying it were killed. It was an awful sight to see two bodies with parts blown off, and it is something that has stayed with me since that night.'

He stayed in the Ulster Defence Regiment for five years and then decided that he would like to change to the Royal Ulster Constabulary Reserve; his father stayed with the Ulster Defence Regiment. 'Again I spent a lot of time in the police station doing security and gate duties and it was there that I had the first narrow escape of my life,' said Norman.

He and a colleague were opening and closing the gates to allow various security vehicles in and out of the compound. On 4 July 1978, while the gates were open during one of these instances, a car, carrying members of the IRA, drove past, and the occupants raked the barracks with gunfire.

'My colleague was hit and fell to the ground in front of me; he had been killed instantly and, unfortunately, his killers got away. I ran to my friend, but there was nothing that I could do for him.'

No one offered Norman any sort of help or counselling at the time, or even suggested that he should go home for the rest of the night. Instead, with the sight of his friend being murdered clearly etched on his mind, he had to carry on working.

As the violence continued and the bombings and murders continued, seemingly unabated, Norman continued to serve in the RUC Reserve, but gradually the sights that he had seen were beginning to take their toll. 'I began drinking and smoking between sixty and eighty cigarettes a day but didn't realise, as yet, just what exactly was the matter.'

His relationship with his father still continued and, as he did for all of his children, William visited often, bringing fresh vegetables that he had grown for them and, despite their married status, he still provided for them where he could. 'He was the heart of our family, still looking after us and doing what he could to help us.'

On Sunday 3 August 1980 his father was in Norman's house having lunch when a neighbour from across the street called to see him. 'The neighbour said that he had just received a telephone call to say that some of the cattle that my father had in a field at Pettigo were ill and he would need to go and see to their needs.'

Pettigo is a village that straddles the border between Northern Ireland and the Republic and part of it is in each State. The cattle were in a field that William leased on the Republic's side and he visited there often to attend to the animals. 'When he heard the message, he said that he would go right away and, around one o'clock, he left my house to go and check on them.'

After his father had left, Norman and one of his cousins went to the nearby River Derg to fish as they had arranged previously; he thought no more of his father's mission to see his cattle because it was a regular journey.

'We were standing in the river fishing at about four thirty that day when I heard someone calling me and saw that it was my next door neighbour. He said that I was wanted urgently at the police station and that I was to go immediately. All sorts of things were going through my head and I thought that something had happened to one of my children. I went as fast as I could to see what the reason was.'

When he reached the station, he was met at the gate by two senior officers who told him that his father had been shot. Norman asked if he was dead and was told that he was.

'My father had gone to check on his cattle and it seems that an ambush had been set up to wait for him. The road that he had to take to the field was not a great road and to manoeuvre the bends he could only have been travelling at about ten miles an hour. It was about two o'clock when he was ambushed by three gunmen who had fired at least fifty bullets from AK47 rifles at the Morris Minor car in which he was travelling.'

When Norman arrived at the scene, his two brothers and brother-in-law were already there; he was asked if he wanted to see his father's body. 'He had been shot nine times in the back of the head, his arm had been shot off and, altogether, there were around forty bullets in his body.'

That was not the end of the horror, however, as the authorities in the Republic did not allow the body to be moved until eleven o'clock the next day.

'It was a day and a half from the time he was shot until we could bring his body back home, that was a terrible experience to know that our father was lying there all of that time and we could do nothing. It was worse to know that we had lost our father and the person who was the heart of us all and who had provided for us all of his life. The IRA issued a statement to say that he was murdered because he was part of the British war machine.'

On the day of his funeral William was buried with full military honours following a service in the local Presbyterian Church. This was the man who was going to tend to sick animals and who lost his life in an ambush by three gunmen and with no means of defending himself. This was the man who worked to protect the family and country he loved and who was shot over forty times by the enemies of democracy who saw him as a threat to their killing campaign.

Because he had been the last member of the family to see him alive, Norman was called on to attend the court case of his father's murderers in Dublin, and when he said that he didn't want to go, he was told that if he didn't go voluntarily he would be arrested and taken.

'My brother and I spent two weeks there listening to evidence and, at the end of it, all the accused got was five years for stealing a car that was used in the killing and that was because of the evidence of a nun. There was no substantial evidence against him.'

Following the death of his father, Norman began sinking deeper into himself and still there were no offers of help or counselling or any type of therapy for the trauma he had come through, but he still continued to work to provide for his family.

On 21 November 1988 he was given the duty of manning a barrier in the town that was used to prevent car bombs getting into the shopping area. His colleague that night was his uncle, Reserve Constable William Montieth, and the two took turn about opening and closing the barrier to allow cars out.

'I was in the security box on a high chair and he was outside letting a car through when I heard a loud bang and I thought that it was a tyre bursting. Then there was another bang and, as I got up to go and see what it was, a gunman appeared at the door of the security box and stood with a gun pointing at me. My immediate reaction was to go for him and the gun; I must have caught my hand on the point of the gun, I pushed it away from me just as he fired. My hand must have caught in the mechanism of the gun as I had a cut on the side. The first gunman then ran down the street. As I went out of the security box, I remember a flash and a burning sensation in my head. The bullet from the gun grazed the top of my head and left a channel cut right along the top and powder marks because it had been so close to me.'

It was a second gunman that had fired, and when he too ran down the street, Norman ran outside to see his uncle lying on the street and knew that he was dead. As other people arrived on the scene, so did Norman's young cousin, the son of the murdered uncle who had been cold-bloodedly killed on the street while opening a barrier to allow his killers to leave the town centre.

'I will never forget him kneeling beside his father and rubbing his hand on his stomach and talking to him, it was heartbreaking and I can still see that scene to this day,' he recalls.

When the ambulance arrived to take the casualties to hospital, William Montieth's body was put in first and Norman had to go in the same ambulance to the hospital. 'That was a terrible experience, travelling in the same ambulance as my uncle who had been murdered in front of me.'

It was shortly after this, and probably because of seeing the murder, that Norman began slipping into a depression which was to last for a long time. 'It was like going into a tunnel and I didn't know what was happening to me. I was still drinking and smoking and could neither explain nor deal with what was happening. I was a very changed man. I was off work for seven months following that shooting and felt that I needed to get back as it would help me deal with the feelings that I was having.'

Initially, his superiors said that they would not send him back on barrier duty but Norman requested that they did, as he needed to put the memories of that shooting behind him so that he could perhaps deal with life a little better. For the next eight years he continued to work as usual, providing a much needed service to a beleaguered community who had suffered so much at the hands of terrorists but was still haunted by many scenes from the past and which now affected his present.

In 1996, following a fall at his work Norman's working career came to an end, but not the problems and stress that he inherited along the way. 'I was having great difficulties in dealing with my life, the slightest thing could trigger flash backs and I couldn't deal with many situations. Things like a scene in a film would bring the memories flooding back and I would have to leave the room that I was in to get away from the recollections.'

One evening while they were sitting at home, Norman and his wife Grace were watching the television and suddenly Norman, for no apparent reason, hit a vase that was sitting on a table beside him and the force sent it along the living room. It shattered at the far end of the room and the incident, along with startling Grace, was the deciding factor that Norman needed professional help.

'I knew for a long time that he was having problems and that Norman was not his usual self. This was something that he had never done before and it was obvious that his condition was getting worse,' said Grace. 'We, the family, watched him change and no one in the police seemed to have noticed or were interested. Many wives have to suffer with their husbands and watch them deal with the horrors they have been through, they don't seem to count either.'

He eventually agreed to see his family doctor who told him that he was suffering from Post Traumatic Stress and would need some professional help to get through it. 'I was sent to see a doctor whom I knew and found it difficult to talk openly to him and so I wasted a few more years; we both knew that I was not improving.'

The problem that Norman felt he had was that no effort or offer had been made during his service years to allow him to see someone who could help with the trauma he had experienced. No one ever talked through the murder attempt on his life or how he was dealing with the loss of his colleagues or his father.

Thomas Loughlin
31 March 1939 – 2 March 1984

Castlederg is not a very big place but, in proportion to its population, it has had a higher percentage of murders than almost anywhere else in Northern Ireland. In some instances more than one member of a family has lost their life in the terror campaign that waged for over thirty years.

The heartache felt by the families of all those who lost their lives was and is both terrible and devastating, but multiplied many fold when visited on them again.

Elma Kerrigan met her future husband when out on a social evening in a local bar. Thomas Loughlin was there as well and, as the evening progressed, the two had struck up a conversation and, by the end of the evening, he had asked for a date. 'I remember when he called our home to talk to me he asked my mother if he could speak to Wilma, she told him that there was no Wilma living there – it took a while to sort the confusion out. Not a very good start, but we laughed about it afterwards,' remembered Elma.

From that first meeting the two built a solid relationship and their romance deepened. The following year Thomas asked Elma to come with him on a visit to Canada to meet and be introduced to other members of his family. 'We went for three weeks and, although it was a beautiful country, I had never before been very far from Castlederg and I felt really homesick. I didn't even call home until the day before we were coming back as I knew that if I heard their voices I would have wanted to come home straight away.'

Thomas had made a great impression on Elma however, and their romance grew stronger and her feelings for him grew as well. 'He was very easygoing and very kind. He never criticised or offended anyone and those were some of the things that I liked about him.'

It was not all plain sailing as Thomas was a divorcee with a family from his previous marriage and, when the time came when he asked Elma to marry him, there was a problem. 'My church, the Church of Ireland, would not marry us because he was a divorcee and, at that time, they did not marry a divorced person. We had to get married in the Presbyterian Church, it was a nice ceremony and we still ended up married.'

Thomas worked with the Department of the Environment Water Division and was a part-time member of the Ulster Defence Regiment.

'He was a great provider for his family, his children always came first and he was also a very homely man, never wanting to be going places, but was happy just being at home. We used to go somewhere for a drive on a Sunday because of his working hours and being on patrol with the UDR and both of us were happy with that time we had.'

Like the other wives who stayed at home while their husbands patrolled the countryside into the small hours of the mornings in an effort to maintain law and order and to curb the terrorist threat, Elma had her fears as well.

'I worried about him when he went on patrol three evenings a week, but never thought that it could ever happen to me. Those nights before I went to bed and he was on duty I always looked out of the window across the countryside and wondered where he was and wished him well,' she said.

As part of the requirements of his work with the Department of the Environment, Thomas needed a van and every morning he would check underneath it to ensure that there was no bomb attached to it. 'He always did this, he would open the van, get into the driver's seat, and holding on to the steering wheel, would lean out and look underneath to all those places where a bomb would be placed,' said Elma.

Thus their life continued and soon into their marriage they had a baby girl, both of them delighted in her arrival.

'Thomas was always thinking of things for the home and I remember one November, just before our first Christmas together, we went shopping and he saw a Christmas tree on sale at one shop. We ended up buying it and when we came home he wanted to put it up to see what it looked like and, needless to say, it stayed up until after Christmas. We had the first Christmas tree in Castlederg that year, weeks before anyone else, but that was Thomas,' she smiled.

On 1 March 1984 Thomas had to work late doing an inspection for his work; when he came home, his coat was covered in mud and Elma took it and cleaned all the mud off it so that it would be clean the next day when he would need it again. The next morning saw a light covering of snow over the town and countryside as he prepared for work. The van had been giving a little bit of trouble, but it had been repaired and so the morning was relatively uneventful as he set off for work.

When he left the house Elma picked their baby daughter off the settee where she had been lying and was about to carry her to the door to wave goodbye to her dad. 'There was an explosion and the glass from the front window shot into the room and large pieces stuck into the settee where the baby had been lying moments before. Just opposite our house was an army barracks and I thought that the explosion had come from there and ran outside with the baby to tell Thomas about it. I never thought that it could have been him.'

When she reached the street it was obvious that the bomb had been in the van and, as the smoke still rose from it, she ran to her husband's aid and could see him still sitting behind the steering wheel.

'Some other neighbours came running as well and I handed the baby to one lady who I knew well and then went to Thomas. He said to me, "I am all right; just help me out of the van." I lifted him from the van and onto the ground. I got his coat and put it over him to keep him warm and he said to me that we were never going to keep that coat clean.'

Thomas had suffered very severe injuries to his lower back and, very soon after the explosion, an ambulance arrived and some of the paramedics who came to assist happened to be friends of his. When they placed him in the ambulance they said that Elma could go with him in the ambulance.

'The neighbour said that she would look after the baby and I went with him to the hospital, still wearing my house slippers, and I had to wait in a room while the doctors dealt with him. I was slightly heartened by the fact that he had been talking to me. It was an awful time and I had never felt so lonely in my life as I waited there.'

A representative of the UDR came to the hospital after the news had reached them of the booby trap bombing and they said that they would send a Greenfinch, a woman private, to stay with Elma and give her support. 'It turned out to be my sister Heather who came and she didn't know that it was me she was coming to sit with.'

Shortly after that her minister arrived, along with one of Thomas' daughters from his first marriage; everyone waited to hear the extent of the injuries and soon they were told that they could go into the treatment room to see him.

'When I walked in, the first thing I noticed was that there were no tubes or drips connected to him and I think then I knew that Thomas had died. I could hear his daughter crying, but it still didn't fully register with me that he was gone. I just kept thinking that the whole thing was unreal and that it couldn't be happening to me. I just couldn't accept it.'

Unfortunately, it was all too real and, as she sat in an anteroom to hear from the doctor, all sorts of thoughts went through Elma's mind. 'I remember there was a small window in the room and a wall outside it. At the end of the wall you could see a little of the grounds and roadway and I thought to myself, this is my life. Just at the end of the wall there was a life there for me, a small life, and the wall is like Thomas' death, it's blocking it.'

Thomas was buried after a service in the Church of Ireland parish church that they had both attended following their wedding and, on the night of his burial, Elma was left alone for the first time since they had married. 'I remember lifting a sweater of his and smelling it so that I could feel close to him, but it was not the same.'

For a long time afterward Elma 'just existed' and all sorts of thoughts went through her mind. Thoughts such as her baby's new life meant that an older life had to go in exchange were coming to her quite often and, along with others, she found life difficult for quite a while. 'I missed Thomas, missed his company, missed the person, and no matter what the Government thought about the UDR, Thomas was a real soldier and I was proud of him for the job he did.'

My sister Heather was a great help to me in those days and she encouraged me to learn to drive and was great company. I owe her a lot. Elma has married again and found the happiness that was taken from her by the terrorist bomb, but she still remembers that day when her world was shattered and changed forever.

Roy Hamilton
4 April 1958 – 14 May 1980

Roy Hamilton was the eldest of the six children of Andy and Peggy Hamilton from the village of Douglas Bridge in County Tyrone. Like most Ulster folk they were hard working, ordinary people who never sought the limelight or to be thrust into the glare of the media; they just wanted to get on with their lives as peacefully and quietly as possible.

That was not be, however, as Roy was gunned down in cold blood while at his work by three killers who fired twenty-one bullets into his body.

He was 'a loveable and kind child who loved sports' as described by his mother, and won many trophies for running while he was still at school. 'While I never felt or made a difference in any of my children, there was an extra spark for Roy, probably because he was the firstborn and because of his nature.'

The family home was a cottage and, during his school days, Roy kept chickens in the back garden that he swapped with other breeders while supplying the family with fresh eggs. He also had a great love of farming and after school would often go to his great uncle's farm three miles away to help with the animals and other chores.

'I think it was then that he developed his love of farming and in later years he leased a field from his grandmother and started keeping cows. Just one or two at first, but when he died he and his brother had seven between them,' said Peggy.

His other love was Gorticlare Pipe Band, a local competition band in which he was a drummer and who won many prizes in local friendly rivalry and, whenever possible, he donned his kilt to march and compete with the others.

'When he was growing up he was a sort of father figure to his younger brothers or sisters and, if they wanted to go somewhere, they always went to Roy and he would come and ask either his father or me if they could go and that he would take them. He was good to them and looked after them well.'

When he reached the age when he could leave school he did so as he was aware that he could help his parents financially in bringing up the rest of the family if he got a job. He had already served his time learning the skill of brick laying and, when he qualified, he lost no time in setting up his own business and seeking work wherever he could get it. 'He was always a very hard worker and, when he got work to do, he employed two of his friends so that they could all work together,' said Peggy.

It was around this time that a new housing estate called Ballymagroarty was being built in Londonderry, just over thirty miles away. Roy had received a contract to do work there and, with his two colleagues, went to earn his wages.

It was also a year when the murder campaign was at its height and news reports every day told of someone being murdered across the Province. Never suspecting that any of them could be a target, the young men carried on with their responsibilities.

On the night of Friday 9 May 1980, the family sat around the dinner table and Roy said to his father that 'a strange thing happened today at work'. He went on to explain that while they worked that day three young men in white shirts had come across the building site directly towards them and stopped to ask where the boss was.

Roy directed them to where the foreman was, but thought that it was strange they had passed other people to come to him to ask. He also mentioned that they had run out of cement that day as the people responsible for making it had not made enough. 'They wouldn't have been doing a dummy run, would they?' he asked.

All that weekend Peggy worried about the possibilities that her son had voiced and she remembered all of the warnings she had given her children.

'I always told them to be careful where they went or what they did in case something happened to them, but I had no real reason to worry about Roy as he was not a member of the security forces, nor was he a member of any paramilitary organisation or anything that would make anyone want to kill him. I still worried about what he had told us all the time.'

The weekend continued as usual and all the family went to their local Presbyterian Church on the Sunday where they had communion and, although nothing further was said about it, the conversation from Friday night was still with Peggy.

On the Monday and Tuesday everyone went to work and returned home as usual and, when Roy appeared home, Peggy had that extra sense of relief. On Wednesday morning while having breakfast Peggy said to one of her daughters: 'I would love to let down the tyres on Roy's car to stop him going to work.' He overheard his mother, and asked: 'What did you say?'

He told her to stop worrying and, after they had all called their goodbyes, everyone left for work. For Peggy that meant another day in Herdmans Linen Mill in Sion Mills where she had worked for many years. Her husband was a bus driver and he too went to his job, as did the older members of the family. Their youngest child was left in the care of a family member.

At 11.45 that day Peggy was working her frame at her workstation when she suddenly felt the sensation of a hand on her right shoulder and a voice said to her: 'Come with me to Londonderry.' She froze where she was and began to feel nauseated, she switched off her frame while she composed herself. When she felt she could move again, she went to a colleague and told her what she had just experienced and who blanched when she listened.

As her lunch break was almost due, Peggy waited until after it was over before she again turned on her machine; she had no sooner done so when her manager came and placed his hand on her shoulder and asked her to come to the office. She kept asking why she had to go with him and what the matter was, his answer was that he would talk in the office.

'When I reached it I saw my husband with one of my daughters and two sons who also worked in the Mill along with two of my sisters-in-law, and it was then that my husband told me that Roy was dead.'

Just around the same time that Peggy had experienced the hand on her shoulder, her son was busy at his work laying the bricks that would provide much needed housing. That day again there had not been enough cement made, just as it had happened on the Friday and had never happened any other day.

The same three young men approached Roy, and called, 'Hi boy' and, thinking they had called 'Hi Roy', he looked around. The three started firing at him and hit him twenty-one times, once in the heart, and the other times in the midriff. Roy died where he fell.

No one ever came to officially tell Peggy or her husband that their son had been murdered. They found out when Andy was about to board the bus he was to drive that day and a colleague came and told him that he should go home as his son had been murdered.

It was he who told Peggy and the rest of the family about what had happened and Peggy's mother heard about it on the radio. No official ever came to tell them or to discuss it with them until the following Saturday when two detectives called to carry out investigations.

'Roy's body came home that night and he was buried after a church service that was attended by all of his friends, and he had a lot. It was a big attendance and I managed quite well until it came to the part where his body was lowered into the ground; I couldn't watch that so I went back inside the church to wait,' said Peggy. 'When the detectives came they asked all sorts of questions about Roy and knew nothing about what happened to him or why. I have to say that I got quite angry at the questions they were asking and I banged the table and told them so.'

When asked if there was anything that they could do for her, Peggy's only request was that she could see the place where her son had been murdered and it was arranged for her to be taken.

'When I went to the place I saw his red pen that I had bought him lying in the mud so I picked it up. I also found his trowel and something else that I can't remember, but I gathered them all up. I remember looking at the mud and thinking that this is where his life was ended and I said, "God bless you, Roy", and then I came away. I have just been back one other time since then and I saw the house built where he died.'

No one has ever claimed responsibility for the murder and no one has ever been charged and, since the visit of the two detectives to the home, no one has ever called back with Peggy or kept her informed what was happening with the investigation, if anything.

In 2004 she began writing to the Police Authority in an attempt to find out the full story of her son's death and any forensic information there might be, such as if the guns had been used in other murders. To date, all she has received is a standard letter outlining a course of action she may follow, but giving no information about the murder.

Peggy has since lost her husband, her mother, and her eldest daughter, and claims that the murder had brought about so much hurt and worry for them all that their health had suffered.

'I sometimes think about the Bible stories I read and realise that Roy has not been taken away from us for good, he has simply gone home and we will meet with him again. I am not a judge, God has told us that we shouldn't judge others. He is the judge and he will punish those who did this. Thou shalt not kill.'

Kingsmills Massacre

It was approximately 5.30 in the evening when a mini van carrying twelve workmen drove through the South Armagh village of Whitecross. Earlier that day at their work, in a textile factory at Glenanne, some of the men had been talking about the murder of the Reavey brothers in the village the day before.

Three brothers, John aged 24, Brian aged 22, and Anthony aged 17 were in their home at Whitecross when gunmen using the name, the Protestant Action Force, forced their way into their home and shot each of them. John and Brian died immediately and Anthony died on the 30 January from the injuries he sustained in the attack.

When the mini van reached the crossroads at Kingsmills, on its way to Bessbrook, where all the workers lived, they were signalled to stop by a group of men on the road in front of the vehicle who were carrying arms; the occupants of the van thought at first that they had come to an army checkpoint.

They were ordered out of the vehicle and it was then that they saw the group of twelve armed men close up, all with their faces blackened, and realised that this was not the army. The only gunman who spoke had an English accent – he asked if there were any Roman Catholics in the group, the only one being the driver and, when he identified himself, he was ordered to go on along the road and not look back.

Once he had gone, the gunmen all opened fire at the remaining Protestant workmen leaving them all for dead on the road. Only one survived despite terrible injuries.

Those murdered were:

Walter Chapman aged 23
Kenneth Worton aged 24, married with 2 children
Reggie Chapman aged 25, married with 2 children
Jim McWhirter aged 58, married with 3 children
John McConville aged 20
Joseph Lemmon aged 46, married with 3 children
John Bryans aged 46, a widower with 2 children who were
left orphaned
Robert Freeburn aged 50, married with 2 children
Robert Chambers aged 19
Robert Walker aged 46

No one was ever brought to trial.

Kenneth Smyth
24 November 1943 – 10 December 1971

Kenneth Smyth loved hunting or anything to do with the outdoors and, as often as possible, spent his time in the fields and countryside around his native Castlederg in County Tyrone.

He was the eldest of four children and described as very talented while at school and with a great ability at hand crafts, especially anything to do with wood.

Being a lot younger than Kenneth, his sister Shelley does not remember much about his earlier years, but she does remember him as being very quiet natured and a person who enjoyed fun.

'Our grandmother and one of our aunts lived at Urney, a little way from where we lived and we used to go there often. Our aunt lived in a small valley near our grandmother's house and to get from her house to our grandmother's we had to walk a steep road. There was a wall around her house and, as we approached it, we would have water fired at us or thrown over us by Kenneth and one of our cousins. We always had water fights every time we went there and they were always instigated by Kenneth,' she remembered.

In later years Kenneth went to stay at his grandparents house and kept his gundogs there so that he could go hunting more easily in the nearby countryside.

Because of the constant terror campaigns being waged in Northern Ireland, security was always of paramount importance and, to supplement the regular police service, the Special Constabulary or B men was formed. Kenneth was a member of this force and carried out regular security duties around the frontiers of Northern Ireland or guarded specific installations against attack.

He was still a member when he decided that he would like to go to Canada and join the Royal Canadian Mounted Police and went over there to follow his ambition. 'It was partially the police and partially the wide open spaces which attracted him,' said Shelley, 'but he only stayed a month as our grandparents, especially my grandmother, pleaded with him to come home as he was missed so much.'

Around the time that he came home the B men had been disbanded and was to be replaced by the Ulster Defence Regiment, so he decided to join up.

'We never worried about him joining as the UDR was for both Protestants and Roman Catholics to join so that the country could be guarded against the men of violence, wherever they came from. Some members of the Roman Catholic faith did join at the beginning but, because of intimidation, they had to leave and any others thinking of joining were discouraged from doing so.'

Shelly also recalled her childhood at home when terrorism was rife and security measures were a formality for many families who supported the forces of law and order. 'We lived beside the police station in Castlederg and, because of the number of attacks being carried out on other police stations across the country, there was always the fear of the same thing happening here.'

In many instances, the IRA or INLA commandeered houses near these establishments so that homemade rockets or mortar bombs could be fired.

'Our father used to sit up some nights to keep watch on all of us and we always had a pile of clean and folded clothes in the bedroom in case we needed to make a fast getaway. There was also a rope under our beds so that we could climb through the window and drop to the street if there was a takeover of the house or bomb damage. It was normal routine for us and we never felt it was unusual,' said Shelly.

While much was done to give the children as normal a life as possible, despite the constant killings in the area, there were times when the family was drawn into the programme of civil disobedience and disruption that was the other part of their campaign.

'My father worked as a meter inspector for the Electricity Service and it was his job to visit homes in his area to read the meters so that the charges could be calculated for each home. In the village of Clady, which is predominantly Republican, he was threatened and told that he was not to come there to do his job. He was not the sort of person who would give in to threats and so he continued to do so. While he did it, Kenneth was lying in nearby fields guarding him to ensure his safety and to make sure that he was not attacked.'

It was in the village of Clady that the first member of the Ulster Defence Regiment was murdered. On 9 August 1971, twenty-two-year-old Winston Donnell was part of a patrol operating a vehicle control point when he was shot. At his funeral, Kenneth drove the vehicle that carried the gun carriage holding Winston's body in the cortege.

At their grandparents house things were a little more difficult as it was known that Kenneth lived there and one night the house was petrol bombed but, thankfully, the flames did not do much damage. To prevent any danger from a similar attack the couple had to cover their windows with wire mesh, but refused to be driven from their home.

When Kenneth was at home in his grandparents he placed his car in the garage and closed and locked the garage door. On the nights that he went out either socially or on business he left the garage door open so that he could drive inside in safety and not provide himself as a target by getting out of his car to open it.

One particular night he was out and, for some unknown reason, he closed the garage door and watchers must have assumed he was at home. A group of masked and armed men attacked the house and forced their way inside. His grandfather was talking on the telephone and this was pulled from the wall by one of the raiders. They made their way straight to Kenneth's bedroom but, on seeing it empty, left the house again and ran off into the darkness.

'Someone knew the layout of the house when they were able to go straight to that particular room and they would have murdered him that night in front of my grandparents if he had been at home,' claimed Shelley.

To underline their intentions, Kenneth began receiving numerous death threats including one in a note form that was left on the windscreen of his Land Rover when it was parked in the nearby town of Strabane. He took the threats seriously enough to take proper precautions and, for months prior to his death, he slept in a different house every night so that he would not have a known routine.

In September 1971 he married Joan and the two of them went to live back at his family home in Castlederg where they took over the top flat in the house so they could have their own lives and routine away from the family.

On the morning of Friday 10 December 1971, Shelly was in the bathroom preparing for school when she heard the young couple coming downstairs to go to their places of work. 'I heard them laughing and talking as they came downstairs and something that I had never done before, I listened for the sound of Kenneth's Land Rover driving off.'

As the day seemed no different to any other, the family carried on their normal routine and Shelley went off to school for the day.

'I remember that I was in my Domestic Science class when I was asked to go to the Headmaster's office. I was thirteen years old at the time. I remember that he took me home in his blue Hillman Imp car and I knew that something bad had happened. I thought that my grandparents house had been attacked again. When the car stopped, I was going to the house and a neighbour called to me that Kenneth had been shot. I dropped my school bag and ran on home.'

Kenneth had his own successful construction business and, on that morning, he had collected one of his workmen to take him to the job they were working on and was on his way to collect a second. They were travelling along Lisdo Road in Clady when they had to stop because of a rope that had been tied across the road. Kenneth stopped the car to reverse away from it, but a number of gunmen began shooting at the vehicle.

His passenger Daniel McCormick was shot and killed and Kenneth was seriously injured. He managed to get outside, but fell onto the ground. While he lay there, he was shot again at close range and died from the injury.

His body was taken to the church where he had been married and was given a fulltime guard until the funeral on the Sunday, when he was buried with full military honours. On the day of the funeral, members of the Official IRA went to Brickfield House, the home of Unionist Senator, Jack Barnhill.

When he opened the door, he was shot twice in the chest. A bomb was then placed beside his body and his wife told that she had three minutes to leave the house.

The bomb exploded and the house was destroyed and, in a follow-up statement, the IRA said that they had not intended to shoot Senator Barnhill but only to destroy the house. They said that he had attempted to grapple with them at the door and this was the reason he was murdered.

While they tried to get on with life as best they could, Shelley remembers that Christmas a few weeks later was one of the saddest days of her life. 'I remember my mother crying the whole day and there was a feeling of gloom over everything. We missed him terribly and Christmas has never been the same for me since.'

Years later, Shelly began her own investigation into what happened to her brother and, from the information available, was told that four men were involved. Three possibly did the shootings and the other was the driver of the car to help their getaway.

'I know that two of them are dead now and the other two are living in the Republic of Ireland. I have also written in depth to Prime Minister Tony Blair regarding his recent announcement that all unsolved murders from the past thirty years would be reinvestigated. I have received a three-line reply stating that my letter had been received.'

To date, there has not been anyone brought to justice for Kenneth's murder and Shelly still has strong feelings about her brother's death. 'I just can't forgive them for what they did as they have taken so much from us. We are the people who are living life sentences, but even if they had received a prison sentence, I don't think that I would have been satisfied. If these people who were known murderers had received the death sentence at the start of the Troubles then less people would have been murdered. Where there is conclusive proof of guilt, then it should be a life for a life.'

As it is, Shelly has fond memories to help her through the bad times; 'I remember a tall, dark, handsome man who will be forever twenty seven years of age.'

William David Brown
12 May 1958 – 13 March 1977

Throughout all the years of the terrorist murder campaign in Northern Ireland the media have been consistent in covering the killings with as much clarity as they could glean before going to press with their covering articles.

While in many cases some reporters took time to gain the facts and a degree of insight into the life and individuality of the latest victim, there were times when statistics were all that was explained about the person whose life had been cruelly and inexcusably taken.

As the death toll rose there were increasing incidences when the victim was referred to as the fifty-ninth member of the Ulster Defence Regiment to lose his or her life, the twentieth civilian or the eightieth member of the regular army and here they would name the regiment.

This anonymity did not give a background to the individual or make public the personality of the statistic they had become, but who had given his or her life in the service of the whole community.

Each and every number in the rolls of honour of the Royal Ulster Constabulary, the Royal Ulster Constabulary Reserve, The Ulster Defence Regiment or the regular army was a person who had hopes, ambitions, abilities, loved ones, and a right to have carried on with fulfilling whatever dreams they had in their lives. Any one of these statistics had a history and a personality which was unique to them but which gave them the right to be remembered and known for the sacrifice that they made.

Constable William David Brown was such a person and as a statistic he was the one hundredth policeman to be murdered in the terror campaign in Northern Ireland, but more than that, he was a person who had so much to live for.

He was born on May 12 1958, the youngest boy of David and Martha Brown in the village of Castlederg; he had two older brothers and a younger sister.

In his youth William was a happy-go-lucky young man with a lot of friends whom he enjoyed going out with. He was educated at Erganagh Primary School and then Castlederg Secondary School, but even before his education was finished, he knew what he wanted to do with his life.

'He always had an interest in joining the Royal Ulster Constabulary and, as soon as he finished school, he joined the RUC Cadets,' said his brother Kenneth.

While still at school he worked for local farmers when school finished for the day and at the weekends. He was a very strong and fit person and at six-foot-three he was an ideal candidate for the Force. As well as his social life with his friends, William's other interest was the local pipe band at Tullywhisker – it was a competition band and one that was quite successful in the many contests it took part in.

'He was sixteen when he joined the Cadets and he really threw himself into it and took part in many of their sporting activities as well as their academic programmes.' So involved was he that he often came home with many bruises and cuts, trophies from his actions with the Cadet rugby team and, on one occasion, a broken collar bone. As he did with everything in life, William gave of his best, even on the sporting field.

In November 1976, after his passing out parade at the police Depot, he was stationed at Tennant Street in Belfast, but was then transferred to Lisnaskea in County Fermanagh.

On Friday 11 March 1977 he was at home in County Tyrone, helping his brother Kenneth build a new house. Kenneth was planning to get married later in the year and William was to be his best man. 'He got a call from his station to say that they were short-staffed that weekend and asked if he could come back early to do some duties. William agreed and that Friday morning he set off back to Lisnaskea.'

On Sunday 13 March at 2.40 p.m. he left Lisnaskea Police Station to go on mobile patrol along with Reserve Constable Robbie Henderson and Woman Constable Lynn Lunney, William was driving. The vehicle they were travelling in was a standard Ford Cortina that in those days did not have any type of armour plating; another unfortunate circumstance was that neither of the radios in the vehicle was working.

A short time later they were ambushed near Ballagh Crossroads by an unknown number of IRA men who fired at the police car with the three personnel inside it. William was critically injured, Reserve Constable Henderson was hit in the right arm and leg but, despite his injuries, he returned fire at their attackers. Policewomen in those days were not armed so Constable Lunney could not return the fire.

Even though wounded, William was able to drive the car away from the ambush area, but it then crashed into a field. Because there were no working radios in the vehicle there was no way they could call for help and they had to wait until their predicament would be noticed.

Other police in the area had heard the shooting and made their way to the scene; a passing motorist who had seen what happened went to the Police Station at Lisnaskea and reported the incident. Although his colleagues gave him first aid and did all they could to save his life, it was forty-five minutes before any help arrived and William had died from his injuries.

He was eighteen years and ten months old, the youngest member of the police to be killed by terrorists and also the one hundredth member of the police to be murdered.

At around six o'clock that evening, Kenneth, his mother, and his sister were sitting at home watching the news on the television. A reporter told of the killing of a policeman in an ambush near Lisnaskea that afternoon.

'A few minutes later my sister ran in and said that there was a police car in the yard and when I went to the door I was met by a Sergeant and a Constable from the local police station,' said Kenneth. 'Our local doctor and the family minister, Canon Northbridge, were also there and they went inside to my mother and sister. William's girlfriend, Kathleen, also arrived, very distraught, and other friends and neighbours came as the news spread. My father, who had been visiting, arrived a short time later to be given the news.'

His funeral took place at Derg Parish Church and, along with Canon Northbridge, Archbishop Robin Eames also officiated at the service which was attended by mourners from all over the Province and from both traditions, a sign of the esteem in which the young constable was held.

At the subsequent inquest into the murder, Kenneth found out that his brother had been shot three times in the back, but despite the injuries he still sought to ensure the safety of his colleagues. Such was the act of heroism that William was posthumously awarded the Queens Gallantry Medal for his efforts to remove his colleagues from the area of the ambush and, in doing so, undoubtedly saved their lives.

Although a number of people were arrested that night and questioned about the murder, no one to date has ever been charged with it and his killers are still free. 'At the time I was very bitter, but I now realise that there are good people on both sides and I try to be a little more tolerant,' said Kenneth.

From the time of the ambush, both of William's colleagues in the car have kept in touch with his parents but, sadly, Reserve Constable Henderson has since died of cancer. 'All of the family greatly appreciated their continued contact with our parents over the years and we have only good thoughts of them both.'

A tragic story but one of immeasurable heroism, which should be remembered, and a life that will never, and should never, be a statistic.

Tracy Doak
17 April 1964 – 20 May 1985

'Tracy was a popular, hard working, and reliable student. She can be pleased with her performance in Ullswater and I am sure she will prove a most able and worthwhile member of the RUC, particularly in the current climate. Overall, an excellent performance by a most mature and impressive young woman whom I assessed with considerable scrutiny against my own, not inconsiderable, firsthand experience of Northern Ireland. She showed concern for and understanding of others, doing much for the group and the success of others less able than herself.'

That was the perceptive opinion of Peter Booth, Deputy Warden of the Outward Bound Mountain School, Ullswater, that Tracy Doak attended in February and March of 1982 when she was seventeen years of age.

Tracy was the second of four children of Beattie and Jean Doak – she had an older brother and two younger sisters. A very happy child, she kept busy with various activities and attending different organisations.

She attended the Hon. Irish Society's Primary School in Coleraine followed by the Coleraine High School for Girls. In her childhood and youth, she was a Brownie and Girl Guide. Music was her passion – she enjoyed piano and singing in her church choir. She was also an enthusiastic and successful Irish dancer and an addictive tapestry worker. Her talent with the needle is still appreciated by her family as Tracy made each a tapestry of their own – something especially valued by them to this day and, along with her memory, is a reminder of what was lost to them.

Despite her many talents, her lifelong wish was to join the Royal Ulster Constabulary, as her father and brother had both been policemen and, a week after she left school at sixteen, she joined the Police Cadets. While there it gave her the opportunity to continue playing sports, which she loved, and she joined their hockey team and went on an Outward Bound Course to Ullswater. Tracy also spent an immensely enjoyable time, as part of her Cadet training, in Thompson House in Lisburn, working with the elderly residents.

'She had an excellent two years in the Cadets and then went on to the RUC training depot at Enniskillen and, following her training, was posted to Newry in County Down,' recalled her mother Jean. 'Tracy was very aware of the risks involved in her new job, but she wasn't frightened and in fact enjoyed the town and the station. I was frightened for her every day she was there and, because she knew this, if there was any type of incident she called home to say that she was alright.'

While serving as a fulltime member of the police, Tracy joined the Christian Police Association and lived her life according to her beliefs. She once told her local minister that, while out on foot patrol in Newry, someone spat on her. In Tracy's words: 'That hurt, because all I wanted to do was my duty and I couldn't understand why a stranger would spit on me.' Despite the rudeness, she still continued to do her duty impartially and as fairly as possible, always with the same temperament and concern for others that she had shown throughout her short life.

On 28 February 1985 the IRA launched a mortar attack on Newry Police Station and nine police officers were killed, among them was Constable Rosemary McGoohan, who was also Tracy's best friend. The others who were also murdered were: Reserve Constable Geoffrey Campbell, Chief Inspector Alexander Donaldson, Sergeant John Dowd, Constable Ivy Kelly, Reserve Constable Paul McFerran, Reserve Constable Sean McHenry, Reserve Constable Denis Price, and Constable David Topping.

When she received a telephone call to report to the Station, Tracy went immediately to see what she could do to help her colleagues; she was visibly unset at the list of casualties that had suffered from the attack. Such a loss, and especially the loss of her best friend, affected Tracy deeply and after that she was not so happy serving in the town as it held too many memories for her.

Just before the tragedy Tracy had become engaged to be married and had built a house in Moira that she had moved into just before Christmas 1984. Her wedding plans were already well advanced – she had chosen her wedding dress, hotel for the reception, and even the music for her big day.

On 12 May 1985 Tracy invited her parents to her home for dinner and they spent one last evening together; Jean took plants for her daughter's garden. 'We had a lovely meal and a lovely time with her. As we left, she stood at the door and waved to us. That was the last time that we saw her alive.'

On 19 May 1985 her brother arrived home from his honeymoon and he, his new bride, and her parents, had all been invited to the family home to have dinner to celebrate the marriage. All the rest of the family were there, but Tracy could not make it due to her own work commitments.

'She was the sort of person who shared in every aspect of our family life, someone who never forgot a birthday or anniversary, and that night she called the house to say hello and welcome home to her brother and his wife. My husband Beattie didn't get to talk with her that night, but she said that there was something that she wanted to talk with him about and that she would call the next day,' recalls Jean.

That next day, Monday 20 May, she called home at around 9.30 a.m. from the canteen in the police station and asked to talk to her father. 'She asked me to advise her of how she could get a transfer from Newry to Antrim and what steps she should take to begin the process,' said Beattie. 'I told her that I would make a few enquiries and let her know and with that she said that she would have to go as she was being called and that she would ring me the next day.'

Tracy had been called to escort a Brinks Matt Security van, which had been travelling from the Republic to Northern Ireland, and it was to be met at the border crossing at Killeen. Along with three colleagues, Constable Ronnie Baird, Reserve Constable Stephen Rodgers, and Inspector William Wilson she set off to the rendezvous point.

When the van crossed the frontier, Tracy manoeuvred her car to take up position in front of it and the other vehicle was to take up the rear. While she turned her car to get into position she had to pass a cattle trailer which had been left at the side of the road. Just as she reached it, the trailer exploded and her car was blown across the road and into a field. Forensics later showed that it had been packed with approximately 1,000 pounds of explosives and had been triggered by remote control from the Republic's side of the border.

All the police personnel were killed in the explosion.

Unaware of what had happened to his daughter, Beattie was cutting a hedge beside his house when he saw a police car make its way towards his house. When it stopped, the two occupants, a Chief Superintendent and a Superintendent, made their way towards him.

'Even before they spoke I knew what they were going to say; I said to them, you are coming to tell me that Tracy is dead. I was numb with shock, but had to go and tell the rest of my family,' he said. 'Despite advice from senior officers I insisted on going to the morgue to identify my daughter. Sometimes I'm glad that I did, but other times I wish that I hadn't. I would rather remember her as Jean and I saw her when we visited her house, standing at the door waving and smiling as she always did.'

Tracy was brought home the next day for her funeral in Ballywatt Presbyterian Church which the family attended regularly and where she had sung in the choir and from where she was buried with full police honours. It was a dull day and among the many who attended was the then Moderator of the Presbyterian Church, Dr Ronald Craig, the Chief Constable, Sir John Hermon, representatives from the Garda Siochana and the Northern Ireland Office.

One of the songs she had requested for her wedding was Chris De Burgh's, In A Country Churchyard. Her mother had suggested that perhaps it wasn't suitable for a wedding as the last verse in particular was very sad. Tracy's response was that they could leave out the last verse and sing the other two. The music to the song was the processional at her funeral and was played by Miss Hilary Lees.

Following her death the family received many letters from friends and strangers alike, and one anonymous letter that they still treasure to this day. It read: 'When I first came to Newry and stepped in among strangers, Tracy was the first one to make me feel welcome. She sat down beside me in the canteen and started to talk. Soon someone else joined in and before long there was a group of people gathered around whom I now call my friends. Just last week I saw her do the same thing to somebody else. That was the kind of person she was, thoughtful, kind, and considerate. She treated everyone the same, whether it was a drunken gypsy or a pompous businessman involved in a traffic accident. She was straightforward, she spoke her mind, she feared no one, and she dealt with people fairly and squarely.'

Another letter from Dublin read: 'As a Catholic family from Dublin we would like you to know that we have never condoned such violence. It is not for Christians to support or condone violence.'

While they are all reminders of the lovely person she was, Jean and Beattie still miss their daughter and especially some of the traits that made her special, such as singing songs and hymns around the piano with her two sisters. 'We as a family miss Tracy so much, the pain is hard to bear; her love and warmth, the infectious laugh, but most of all, we all miss her for the person she was.'

The congregation of Ballywatt Church erected a memorial to Tracy's memory, it was dedicated on the evening of Remembrance Sunday – on the same day that a terrorist bomb exploded at the Cenotaph in Enniskillen.

'We pass her grave every Sunday as we go to worship. In the beginning it was to talk to her as we felt comfortable being there, but now it is just to think and remember,' said Jean.

| Alexander Donaldson | Rosemary McGookin | Geoffrey Campbell | Denis Price | Paul McFerran | Sean McHenry | David Topping | John Dowd | Ivy Kelly |

The nine colleagues of Tracy Doak who were murdered as a result of a mortar bombing attack on Newry Police Station.

138

William Frazer
Families Acting For Innocent Relatives

Along with the murders of loved ones, many families across the Province have also had to deal with other types of intimidation and persecution because their beliefs differed from those of the terrorist. They have been forced to move from the homes they lived in for most of their lives and in their daily routines have had to be constantly aware of the genuine terrorist threat on their lives. Nowhere was this more prevalent than along the border regions of Northern Ireland.

In some isolated regions the systematic murders of one section of the population became general practice and many families lost a number of relatives in what became viewed as an attempt to ethnically cleanse certain areas.

Willie Frazer was born into a Protestant family of nine children in Newry; his father worked as part of the roads maintenance personnel for the local council.

In his early years Willie attended St Mary's Primary School, a Roman Catholic school near their home and while there took part in every activity offered by the school, including playing

Gaelic football. 'I never thought anything about it at the time or realised that I was even at a Roman Catholic school as it was never mentioned at home or that there was a difference.'

However, in 1970, when certain groups within the Republican movement called for a general Rent and Rates strike as part of an ongoing protest action, the situation for the youngster took a more sinister turn.

'As part of the protest we were asked to display a poster in the window saying that we were taking part in the campaign but, being the type of people they were, our parents said that they would not take part as they believed in paying whatever was due to the legal authority,' explained Willie.

Because of their refusal, a campaign of intimidation began against the family, and going to school and coming from it, Willie was regularly beaten up by other pupils. The beatings became so regular and severe that he was eventually taken from the school and moved to Kingsmills Primary School which, although much further away, gave him the security to receive his education in peace.

Their home too was regularly stoned as well as that of their Protestant neighbours next door; the children could not go outside the confines of their garden for fear of attack. 'We eventually had to put up a five-foot barbed wire fence around the house and over the gate into the garden as a type of protection.'

By this time Willie's father had joined the Ulster Defence Regiment, having also served in the B Specials, that was formed by the Government to counteract the increased terrorist threat; he was often out on patrol with his colleagues.

From stones and bricks the next step was a series of no warning bombs and initially there was only minor damage caused to the house, but the threats against the families had risen considerably. These attacks only occurred when his father was out and only women and children were left in the house.

'One night one of my sisters had been sitting outside the house with her boyfriend and when our mother saw her outside she unlocked the front door for her so that she could get into the house quickly. When she got out of her boyfriend's car he came straight into the house and closed the door after her. She had just put the first of the bolts on the door when it was suddenly kicked from the outside. Obviously someone had been outside and was intent on coming into the house after her. We often wondered what their intent was as a bomb exploded outside shortly afterwards.'

The bombs continued, and on one occasion two were placed on the same night blowing part of the roof off the house and causing some minor structural damage. When the family contacted the army they found that no one could come due to a fear of booby traps; the family had to wait until the hours of daylight before a security check could be carried out.

'What they normally did was to contact my father who would have been out on patrol and tell him what had happened and we had to wait. The fourth bomb that was left was a fifteen-pound one at the kitchen window that, thankfully, did not go off. If it had then there would have been serious damage or worse inside the house.'

Despite the intimidation and threat, Willie's father continued to do his duty and would often put on his uniform, take his gun, and meet the patrol further up the road from the house. On those nights that he went on patrol, Willie remembers his mother sitting up all night while she waited on his return so that she could let him into the house and as safely and swiftly as possible.

'In those days it was certainly our mother that kept us together while our father was out on patrol. She is a strong woman and we needed that strength at that time,' he said. 'On one occasion she used our father's 303 rifle to scare off attackers, even though she could not even remove the safety catch.'

The situation for the family deteriorated; eventually they were forced to leave the family home (the neighbours next door had already left) and, following petrol bomb and gun attacks, it was decided that for the children's sake they would move as well.

'The army had to move into our home for three days before we moved out and we had an emergency allocation of a house in Newtownhamilton. It was in a new estate that was being built and had no proper floors but front and back doors were put in for us and for the first month we lived upstairs while the building was completed.'

Following the move the family tried to carry on with life as normally as possible, but what was normal in Northern Ireland at that time? 'One day a friend of mine, William Meaklem, called at the house to say that he was going to make a delivery of gas that had been ordered and then head on to Portrush with friends. He asked me if I wanted to go with him, but I said that I would not go this time and off he went. That was the last time that I ever spoke to him. The IRA captured William and, after they held him captive and tortured him for three days, they dumped his body on the border. William was a civilian and the gas delivery was obviously a trap. I remember being very upset at the funeral and being told by my father that I would need to harden up as there were going to be a lot more funerals before the Troubles were over.'

Tragedy was to come even closer and sooner than anyone wanted or expected when the terrorists targeted his father. 'My father was a hard working, Christian man who read his Bible and knew no fear because of his beliefs. He was often in the graveyard of the church digging graves by lamplight or in the day time looking after the grounds.'

On Saturday 30 August 1975 James Frazer or Bertie, as he was better known, had just finished work and was driving on the outskirts of Markethill when a three-man gang confronted him.

'According to a witness they first tried to kidnap him and pull him out of the car. He put up such resistance that one of them shot him in the back of the head and they then took his car and made their getaway. It took two hours for an ambulance to arrive and by that time my father had bled to death. We subsequently found out that his hands were also broken where he must have held on to the steering wheel to stop them taking him. We are convinced my father fought so hard as he wanted to avoid the fate of William Meaklem.'

Sickeningly, in negotiations after the murder, when the family sought compensation for the car, the Northern Ireland Office told them that their claim should be against their insurers. The insurance company said that they could not pay compensation as the owner of the vehicle was on the scene when it was stolen.

When the body of his father was brought home on the Sunday, many friends and family members called at the house to extend their sympathies and outside there were also some very unwelcome callers. 'Many of my family members were in the security forces by this time and, knowing that they would probably be calling at the house, a number of gunmen were seen approaching our home from the fields at the back.'

The army were called and the group ran back across the fields into the Irish Republic so that they could not be captured. The next night, however, they went to Tullyvallen Orange Hall where they attacked the members and killed five elderly men taking part in a religious service.

Following their father's funeral, the family were still under threat and still refused to move from the house they moved to for sanctuary. 'Five weeks later we came home one night and our mother had packed up the house and said to us that she was moving and we could come if we wanted, of course we went with her. Although we moved to the more secure area of Markethill, our hearts still belong to the home we had to leave in South Armagh.'

Their heartache was not to end with the move, however, and a few months afterwards tragedy hit the family yet again.

Just a few miles up the road from where his father had been murdered, an uncle of Willie's, Johnny Bell, lived on his own in a house that was quite isolated and near a small forest. Johnny lived in his 'home place' without electricity or an inside toilet, simply because it was the home of his birth. He knew that by remaining there he was leaving himself open to the possibility of attack by the IRA. On one of the nights that he was going home he saw some men setting up an ambush and was able to avoid it, he knew that it was meant for him, as he was a part-time member of the Ulster Defence Regiment.

That time the gunmen were chased off, but they returned two weeks later on 6 November 1975. Johnny was driving home in his car that night, but the ambush was set up again and this time he didn't see them. The car was riddled by gunfire and he died immediately from his injuries. Later investigations showed that the gang had been made up mostly from neighbours of the bachelor who lived on his own in the isolated house.

A similar situation brought about the death of Kingsmills man, Clifford Lundy, who had retired from the Ulster Defence Regiment and who worked for a timber merchant in the village. Clifford regularly collected a young man from the area to give him a lift to work and on occasion brought him packed lunches made by his wife. One night when he had finished his work and arrived home he was parking the car when another car drove up beside him and the occupants shot him.

The following investigation showed that the young man to whom he had shown so much kindness and whom he drove to work and whom his wife sent packed lunches had set him up. He was the only one prosecuted for the killing of the Good Samaritan and was given four years imprisonment.

Another cousin of Willie's was shot and killed in Kilkeel and six friends, all in the security forces were also murdered, one of them blown up and the others shot to death.

Following the signing of the Good Friday Agreement, a number of bereaved families could not see the justice in the aftermath when the terrorists who had been captured were given their freedom. Along with many others, Willie felt that if this Agreement was not challenged then all of their loved ones would have died in vain and the families would continue with their life sentences of grief and pain while the perpetrators walked free.

'People kept saying to me that because they had been granted their freedom from punishment that the terrorists would now believe that their cause had been justified. I have become a Christian and believe that justice is important.'

Thus, Families Acting for Innocent Relatives, or FAIR for short, was born and began working to help the relatives of the hundreds who had been murdered in the area, both in a practical way and socially. Their aim is to still bring the many perpetrators of the murders who have escaped the net to justice, and show that they are not immune to the law, as they would feel they are.

'There are still many people afraid to speak out and tell the world what happened to their families in case of retaliation and I feel so sorry for those people who are so frightened. I know that they are dealing with a lot of pain and that goes for victims all over Northern Ireland, but the silence gives reason to those who live in areas which were not affected to say we should now put all of these deaths behind us. I, and many, many others, believe that it is our duty to remember and honour the people who were murdered. These were the brave men and women of this country who put on a uniform and served their country and all too often have been maligned and forgotten for doing so. Some were the ordinary people who served by living normal productive lives, but who worshipped in the wrong way for the terrorist,' said Willie.

The Queen's Speech at the Presentation of the George Cross to the Royal Ulster Constabulary

'I am pleased to be here today on this historic occasion, to present the award of the George Cross to the Royal Ulster Constabulary. This award is an exceptional recognition of the outstanding contribution made by the RUC to peace in Northern Ireland. It is a singular acknowledgement of the gallantry and courage shown and, in all too many cases, the ultimate sacrifice paid by the members of the Constabulary during the past 30 years of terrorism and civil unrest. I want to take this opportunity to pay tribute to all members of the RUC – the regular officers of all ranks, the members of the fulltime and part-time Reserve, and former members who have served so loyally over the years. I salute your courage and your sense of duty. I admire your determination to maintain the rule of law, and to provide a police service for all the people during some of the most difficult times in the history of the Province.

'A terrible price has been paid for this brave and resolute stand.

'We remember today the 302 officers who have lost their lives, and also the many thousands who have been injured, some very seriously, at the hands of terrorists. Their sacrifice must never be forgotten. I also pay tribute to the part played by other, often unsung heroes. It has simply not been possible for officer's families to enjoy normal lives. Today's award recognises the very special contribution made by these families, they have been a constant source of support, and have had to endure fear, intimidation, and worst of all, the pain of bereavement.

'The award also recognises the important part played by civilian colleagues of RUC officers and the Police Authority. And, of course, the RUC have for many years worked alongside the armed forces who themselves have shown that same character of duty we are recognising today.

'Due in no small measure to the bravery and dedication over the years of the men and women of the Royal Ulster Constabulary, Northern Ireland is now a much more peaceful and stable place in which to live. I hope and trust that the enmities of the past can be laid to rest in a way that fully recognises the sacrifices made. I know it is clear to you, as it is to me, that there will be challenges to face in the period of change that lies ahead. I am confident that you will maintain that sense of duty and dedication which is being honoured today. I know also that you will have my support and prayers in the future as the dogged and relentless search for lasting peace continues.'

The Royal Ulster Constabulary
George Cross
Roll of Honour

1969				
Victim Name	*Rank*	*Murdered*	*Murdered By*	*Method Of Murder*
Arbuckle, Victor	Constable	11 October	Loyalists	Shot dead during riot on Shankill Road

1970				
Victim Name	*Rank*	*Murdered*	*Murdered By*	*Method Of Murder*
Donaldson, Sam	Constable	12 August	IRA	Killed by booby trap car bomb in Culloville, Crossmaglen
Millar, Robert	Constable	12 August	IRA	Killed by booby trap car bomb in Culloville, Crossmaglen

1971				
Victim Name	*Rank*	*Murdered*	*Murdered By*	*Method Of Murder*
Buckley, Robert	Constable	28 February	IRA	Shot dead during riots at Alliance Avenue, North Belfast
Patterson, Cecil	D/Inspector	28 February	IRA	Shot dead during riots at Alliance Avenue, North Belfast
Leslie, Robert	Constable	18 September	IRA	Shot and fatally wounded in Castle Place, Strabane
Cunningham, Cecil	Constable	15 October	IRA	Shot dead in Ardoyne, Belfast
Haslett, John	Constable	15 October	IRA	Shot dead in Ardoyne, Belfast
Dodd, Ronald	Sergeant	27 October	IRA	Shot and fatally wounded at Gallagh, Toomebridge
Devlin, Alfred	Inspector	29 October	IRA	Killed in bomb at Chichester Road RUC Station, Belfast
Corry, Stanley	D/Constable	1 November	IRA	Shot dead in Andersonstown, Belfast
Russell, William	D/Constable	1 November	IRA	Shot dead in Andersonstown, Belfast
Hurley, Dermot	Sergeant	11 November	IRA	Fatally injured in gun attack on Oldpark Road, Belfast
Moore, Walter	Constable	11 November	IRA	Fatally injured in gun attack on Oldpark Road, Belfast

			1972	
Victim Name	**Rank**	**Murdered**	**Murdered By**	**Method Of Murder**
Denham, Raymond	R/Constable	12 January	IRA	Shot dead at his civilian employment in factory at Waterford Street, Belfast
Gilgunn, Peter	Sergeant	27 January	IRA	Fatally wounded in gun attack at junction of Creggan Hill/Helen Street, Londonderry
Montgomery, David	Constable	27 January	IRA	Fatally wounded in gun attack at junction of Creggan Hill/Helen Street, Londonderry
Carroll, Raymond	Constable	28 January	IRA	Shot dead as he repaired his car in a garage on Oldpark Road, Belfast
Morrow, Thomas	Sergeant	2 March	IRA	Died from gunshot wounds following gun attack in Newry Road, Camlough, Co Armagh
Logan, William	Constable	15 March	IRA	Died from gunshot wounds following attack in Coalisland, Co Tyrone
McAllister, Ernest	Constable	20 March	IRA	Killed by car bomb as they helped clear civilians from Donegal Street, Belfast
O'Neill, Bernard	Constable	20 March	IRA	Killed by car bomb as they helped clear civilians from Donegal Street, Belfast
Houston, David	Constable	26 June	IRA	Shot and fatally wounded in Newry. He was posthumously awarded the Queen's Police Medal.
Laverty, Robert	Constable	16 July	IRA	Fatally wounded during gun attack on Antrim Road, Belfast
Gibson, Robert	R/Constable	21 July	IRA	Killed by car bomb at Oxford Street bus station
Harron, Gordon	Constable	21 October	Loyalists	Died from gunshot wounds in attack on Shore Road, Belfast. He was posthumously awarded the Queen's Police Medal.
Calvin, Joseph	R/Constable	16 November	IRA	Killed by booby trap car bomb in Enniskillen
Keys, Robert	Constable	28 November	IRA	Killed during rocket attack on Belleek RUC Station
Nixon, James	Constable	13 December	IRA	Shot dead off duty as he left Antrim Road
Chambers, George	Constable	15 December	Official IRA	Fatally injured in gun attack in Kilwilkie Estate, Lurgan, Co Armagh

		1973		
Victim Name	Rank	Murdered	Murdered By	Method Of Murder
Dorset, David	Sergeant	14 January	IRA	Killed in booby trap car bomb in Harbour Square, Londonderry
Sandford, Henry	R/Constable	14 January	IRA	Fatally injured in a landmine explosion on Ballygawley/Cappagh Road, Co Tyrone
Wilson, Mervyn	Constable	14 January	IRA	Killed in booby trap car bomb in Harbour Square, Londonderry
Morrison, Charles	Constable	8 February	IRA	Shot dead in gun attack Donaghmore, Dungannon, Co Tyrone
Wylie, Raymond	Constable	27 February	IRA	Fatally wounded in gun attack at Aghagallon, Aghalee, Co Antrim. He was posthumously awarded the Queen's Police Medal
McCauley, Robert	Constable	25 March	IRA	Fatally wounded in gun attack at Aghagallon, Aghalee, Co Antrim. He was posthumously awarded the Queen's Police Medal
Purvis, David	Constable	5 June	IRA	Fatally wounded in gun attack in Enniskillen
McElveen, William	R/Constable	13 August	IRA	Fatally wounded in gun attack in Cathedral Road, Armagh
Campbell, William	R/Constable	16 October	IRA	Fatally wounded in gun attack on Antrim Road, Belfast
Doherty, John	D/Constable	28 October	IRA	Shot dead in gun ambush as he visited his mother's home at Ballindrait, Lifford, Co Donegal
Megaw, Robert	Constable	1 December	IRA	Shot dead in gun attack at junction of Sloan Street/Edward Street, Lurgan
Rolston, Maurice	Constable	11 December	IRA	Killed in booby trap car bomb outside his home in Newcastle, Co Down
Logue, Michael	Constable	29 December	UDA	Fatally wounded in gun attack Forthriver Road, Belfast

1974				
Victim Name	*Rank*	*Murdered*	*Murdered By*	*Method Of Murder*
Rogers, John	R/Constable	26 January	IRA	Fatally wounded in gun attack in Glengormley, Co Antrim
Baggley, William	R/Constable	29 January	IRA	Fatally wounded in gun attack in Dungiven Road, Londonderry
McClinton, Thomas	Constable	2 March	IRA	Shot dead at point blank range in Upper Donegal Street, Belfast
Wilson, Cyril	Constable	17 March	Loyalists	Fatally wounded in gun attack at junction of Tullygally Road, Ardowne Roundabout, Craigavon, Co Armagh
Robinson, Frederick	Sergeant	19 March	IRA	Killed by booby trap car bomb at his home in Greenisland, Co Antrim
McCall, Thomas	Constable	16 April	IRA	Fatally wounded in gun attack in Newtown-hamilton, Co Armagh
Bell, Brian	Constable	10 May	IRA	Fatally wounded in gun attack at Finaghy Cross Roads
Ross, John	Constable	10 May	IRA	Fatally wounded in gun attack at Finaghy Cross Roads
Forsythe, John	Constable	18 June	IRA	Killed by bomb in car on Market Street, Lurgan
O'Connor, Daniel	Sergeant	22 June	IRA	Fatally wounded in gun attack in Crumlin Road, Belfast
Flannagan, Peter	D/Inspector	23 August	IRA	Fatally wounded by gunmen who singled him out in premises in George's Street, Omagh
Elliott, William	Inspector	6 September	IRA	Fatally wounded as he challenged armed raiders at bank in Rathcoole, Newtownabbey, Co Antrim. He was posthumously awarded the Queen's Police Medal.
McNeice, David	Constable	14 December	IRA	Shot dead in gun attack at Killeavey, Co Armagh

		1975		
Victim Name	*Rank*	*Murdered*	*Murdered By*	*Method Of Murder*
Coulter, George	Sergeant	31 January	IRA	Shot dead in gun attack at junction of Dungannon/ Donoghmore Road, Co Tyrone
Harrison, Mildred	R/Constable	16 March	UVF	Killed by bomb as she and a colleague performed beat duty in Bangor, Co Down
Gray, Paul	Constable	10 May	IRA	Fatally wounded in gun attack on Derry's Wall, Londonderry
Davis, Noel	Constable	24 May	INLA	Killed by booby trap bomb in stolen vehicle at Ballinahone Road, Maghera, Co Londonderry
Johnston, Andrew	D/Constable	7 July	IRA	Killed by booby trap bomb as he examined the scene of a burglary at a school in Sloan Street, Lurgan
McPherson, Robert	Constable	26 July	INLA	Fatally wounded in gun attack in Dungiven, Co Londonderry. He was posthumously awarded a Queen's Commendation for bravery.
Love, David	D/Constable	6 October	IRA	Killed by booby trap bomb at Terrydromond, Limavady, Co Londonderry
Baird, Andrew	R/Constable	14 October	IRA	Fatally wounded by bomb placed at security hut at Church Street, Portadown
Clements, Joseph	R/Constable	16 November	IRA	Fatally wounded in landmine explosion near Cloghfin, Sixmilecross, Co Tyrone
Clarke, Samuel	R/Constable	25 November	IRA	Fatally wounded in gun attack at Clonavaddy, Dungannon, Co Tyrone
Maxwell, Patrick	Sergeant	25 November	IRA	Fatally wounded in gun attack at Clonavaddy, Dungannon, Co Tyrone

1976				
Victim Name	*Rank*	*Murdered*	*Murdered By*	*Method Of Murder*
Evans, Clifford	R/Constable	5 January	IRA	Fatally wounded in gun attack between Toomebridge/Castledawson, Co Londonderry
Bell, George	Inspector	22 January	Unknown	Killed by a booby trap bomb at Donegal Pass RUC Station, Belfast
Cummings, Neville	Constable	22 January	Unknown	Killed by a booby trap bomb at Donegal Pass RUC Station, Belfast
Blakely, James	Sergeant	6 February	IRA	Fatally injured in gun attack near Cliftonville Circus, Belfast
Murtagh, William	Inspector	7 February	IRA	Fatally injured in gun attack near Cliftonville Circus, Belfast
Hamer, William	R/Constable	12 February	IRA	Fatally wounded in gun attack in Claudy, Co Londonderry
Crooks, William	R/Constable	23 April	IRA	Fatally wounded in gun attack at Dernagh Crossroads, Coalisland, Co Tyrone
Evans, Thomas	R/Constable	15 May	IRA	Fatally wounded when a booby trap bomb exploded near Belcoo RUC Station, Co Fermanagh
Hunter, James	Sergeant	15 May	IRA	Fatally wounded in gun attack near Warrenpoint, Co Down
Kettles, Francis	R/Constable	15 May	IRA	Fatally wounded when a booby trap bomb exploded near Belcoo RUC Station, Co Fermanagh
Keys, Harry	Sergeant	15 May	IRA	Fatally wounded when a booby trap bomb exploded near Belcoo RUC Station, Co. Fermanagh
Nelson, Kenneth	R/Constable	16 May	IRA	Shot dead as he let his dog out at his home at Dungannon, Co Tyrone

1976 continued				
Victim Name	*Rank*	*Murdered*	*Murdered By*	*Method Of Murder*
McCambridge, John	Constable	22 May	IRA	Off duty, he was ambushed and shot dead as he stepped out of his car at Corrainey, Dungannon
Baggley, Linda	R/Constable	2 June	IRA	Fatally injured in a gun attack in Chapel Road, Londonderry. Her father who was also in the RUC was killed in 1974.
McAdam, Ronald	D/Constable	2 June	IRA	Off duty, he was shot dead as he collected friends outside the Royal Victoria Hospital, Belfast.
Cush, Thomas	Constable	31 July	IRA	Shot dead at security barrier at Church Place, Lurgan
Armour, James	Constable	26 August	IRA	Not listed
Heaney, James	Constable	26 August	IRA	Off duty, he was working on his car at his mother's house in Andersonstown when he was fatally wounded in gun attack.
Craig, Albert	Sergeant	18 September	IRA	Fatally wounded in gun attack at Shamrock Park, Portadown
McKay, Arthur	R/Constable	8 October	IRA	Killed in booby trap bomb at Drumsaragh Road, Kilrea, Co Londonderry
McCabe, Noel	D/Constable	2 November	IRA	Fatally wounded in gun attack at junction of Clonard Street/Falls Road, Belfast
Scott, Joseph	R/Constable	3 December	IRA	Engaged in his civilian employment as traffic warden, he was shot dead at the junction of Circular Road/Killyman Road, Dungannon, Co Tyrone
Campbell, Norman	Constable	15 December	IRA	Fatally wounded in gun attack at High Street, Portadown
Armour, Samuel	R/Constable	22 December	IRA	Killed when booby trap bomb exploded underneath his car at Maghera, Co Londonderry

		1977		
Victim Name	*Rank*	*Murdered*	*Murdered By*	*Method Of Murder*
Greer, James	R/Constable	14 January	IRA	Killed by booby trap car bomb at his home in Portglenone, Co Antrim
McNulty, Patrick	D/Constable	27 January	IRA	Shot dead as he left his car for service at garage in Strand Road, Londonderry
Harrison, Robert	R/Constable	5 February	IRA	Fatally wounded in gun attack in Gilford, Co Down
McKane, Samuel	R/Constable	17 February	IRA	Fatally wounded in gun attack at his home at Cloughmills, Co Antrim
Cobb, Harold	Inspector	24 February	IRA	Fatally wounded in gun attack at Church Place, Lurgan, Co Armagh
Campbell, Joseph	Sergeant	25 February	Unknown	Shot dead as he closed the gates to Cushendall RUC Station, Co Antrim
Brown, William	Constable	13 March	IRA	Fatally wounded in gun attack between Ballagh Crossroads and Lisnaskea, Co Fermanagh
McCracken, John	Constable	8 April	IRA	Fatally wounded in gun attack on the Moneymore Road, Magherafelt, Co Londonderry
Sheehan, Kenneth	Constable	8 April	IRA	Fatally wounded in gun attack on the Moneymore Road, Magherafelt, Co Londonderry
North, Robert	R/Constable	20 May	RA	Was engaged in his civilian employment as bus driver when he was fatally injured in gun attack at Drumderg, Benburb, Co Tyrone
Davison, Samuel	Constable	2 June	IRA	Fatally wounded in gun attack at Ardboe, Co Tyrone
Lynch, Norman	Constable	2 June	IRA	Fatally wounded in gun attack at Ardboe, Co Tyrone
Martin, Hugh	R/Constable	2 June	IRA	Fatally wounded in gun attack at Ardboe, Co Tyrone
Morrow, David	R/Constable	6 July	IRA	Fatally wounded in gun attack at Aughnacloy, Co Tyrone

		1978		
Victim Name	*Rank*	*Murdered*	*Murdered By*	*Method Of Murder*
Crothers, Gordon	R/Constable	17 February	IRA	One of 12 people killed in blaze which followed a bomb explosion at the La Mon House, Castlereagh, Co Down
Simpson, Charles	Constable	28 February	IRA	Fatally wounded in gun attack at Clarendon Street. Londonderry
Moore, John	R/Constable	15 April	IRA	Killed by landmine under his car at his home near Armoy, Co Antrim
McAllister, Millar	Constable	22 April	IRA	Shot dead at his home in Lisburn, Co Antrim
Struthers, Robert	R/Constable	16 June	IRA	Shot dead at his civilian employment in shop at Lorne Street, Londonderry
McConnell, Hugh	Constable	17 June	IRA	Fatally wounded during gun attack on Camlough/Crossmaglen Road
Turbitt, William	A/Constable	17 June	IRA	Abducted after gun attack on Camlough/Crossmaglen Road. His body was recovered three weeks later at Cullyhanna.
Rankin, Jacob	R/Constable	4 July	IRA	Fatally wounded in gun attack outside Castlederg RUC Station
Lamont, John	R/Constable	2 August	IRA	Fatally wounded in gun attack in George Street, Ballymena
Donaghy, Howard	R/Constable	11 September	IRA	Off duty, he was fatally wounded as he worked at his house at Loughmacroary, Omagh

		1979		
Victim Name	**Rank**	**Murdered**	**Murdered By**	**Method Of Murder**
Baird, Richard	Constable	17 April	IRA	Killed in a booby trap van bomb at Millvale Road, between Bessbrook and Newry.
Gray, Paul	Constable	17 April	IRA	Killed in a booby trap van bomb at Millvale Road, between Bessbrook and Newry
Lockhart, Robert	R/Constable	17 April	IRA	Killed in a booby trap van bomb at Millvale Road, between Bessbrook and Newry.
Webb, Noel	Constable	17 April	IRA	Killed in a booby trap van bomb at Millvale Road, between Bessbrook and Newry
Prue, Norman	D/Constable	6 May	IRA	Shot dead outside Holy Cross Chapel, Chapel Brae, Lisnaskea
Wray, Stanley	R/Constable	20 May	IRA	Fatally wounded in gun attack as he and his family arrived to attend morning service at Claremont Presbyterian Church, Londonderry
Dunne, Alan	R/Constable	2 June	INLA	Fatally wounded in gun attack outside his home in Armagh
Hanna, Stanley	Supt.	3 June	IRA	Killed by bomb near community centre Clonalig, Crossmaglen
Thompson, Keith	Constable	3 June	IRA	Killed by bomb near community centre Clonalig, Crossmaglen
Scott, John	R/Constable	22 June	IRA	Engaged in his civilian employment he was fatally wounded in gun attack at Ardboe, Coagh
Walsh, George	Constable	31 July	INLA	Fatally wounded in gun attack outside Armagh Courthouse
Davidson, Derek	Constable	2 August	IRA	Fatally wounded in gun attack at Clondara Street, Falls Road, Belfast
Davidson, Gerry	Constable	18 November	IRA	Fatally wounded in gun attack at Springfield Road RUC Station, Belfast
Hazelton, Stanley	R/Constable	22 December	IRA	Off duty, he was fatally wounded in gun ambush at Glasslough, Co Monaghan

		1980		
Victim Name	*Rank*	*Murdered*	*Murdered By*	*Method Of Murder*
Crilly, Robert	R/Constable	3 January	IRA	Fatally wounded in gun attack in Newtownbutler, Co Fermanagh
Purse, David	R/Constable	12 January	IRA	Fatally wounded in gun attack at Seaview Football Club, Shore Road, Belfast
Howe, Winston	Constable	11 February	IRA	Killed in landmine explosion at Lisnaskea
Rose, Joseph	Constable	11 February	IRA	Killed in landmine explosion at Lisnaskea
Montgomery, Bernard	R/Constable	4 April	IRA	Fatally wounded in gun attack at Ligoneil, Belfast
Magill, Stephen	Constable	9 April	IRA	Fatally wounded in gun attack at Stewartstown Road, Belfast
Wilson, Fred	R/Constable	11 April	IRA	Shot dead as he arrived at his civilian employment in Franklyn Street, Belfast
Allen, Wallace	R/Constable	1 September	IRA	Ambushed and abducted as he drove his milk lorry in Newtownhamilton area. His body was recovered twelve days later.
Johnston, Ernest	R/Constable	22 September	IRA	Fatally wounded in gun attack outside his home in Lisrace, Magheraveely, Co Fermanagh

		1981		
Victim Name	*Rank*	*Murdered*	*Murdered By*	*Method Of Murder*
McDougall, Lindsay	R/Constable	14 January	INLA	Fatally wounded in gun attack in Great Victoria Street, Belfast
Stronge, James	R/Constable	21 January	IRA	Fatally wounded in gun attack at his home, Tynan Abbey, Co Armagh
Lewis, Charles	R/Constable	6 February	IRA	Fatally wounded in gun attack at Balmoral Avenue, Belfast
Scott, Alexander	R/Constable	8 February	IRA	Fatally wounded in gun attack outside his wife's shop at My Lady's Road, Belfast
Acheson, Kenneth	Constable	2 April	IRA	Fatally wounded in booby trap car bomb at Berry-willigan Road, Bessbrook
Martin, Gary	Constable	27 April	INLA	Killed in booby trap bomb at Shaw's Road, Belfast
Ellis, Philip	Constable	6 May	IRA	Fatally wounded in gun attack at Edlingham Street/Duncairn Gardens, Belfast
Vallely, Samuel	Constable	14 May	IRA	Fatally wounded in rocket grenade attack at Upper Springfield Road, Belfast
Robinson, Mervyn	Constable	28 May	IRA	Off duty, he was shot dead at Whitecross, Co Antrim.
Dunlop, Colin	R/Constable	31 May	IRA	Shot dead while he was on security duty at intensive care unit Royal Victoria Hospital
Kyle, Christopher	R/Constable	17 June	IRA	Off duty, he was fatally wounded in gun attack at his home near Omagh
Quinn, Neal	Constable	20 June	IRA	Off duty, he was fatally wounded in gun attack in North Street, Newry
Smyth, John	Constable	2 August	IRA	Killed when a landmine exploded near Loughmacrory, Omagh
Woods, Andrew	Constable	2 August	IRA	Killed when a landmine exploded near Loughmacrory, Omagh
Evans, Mark	Constable	7 September	IRA	Killed in landmine explosion near Pomeroy
Montgomery, John	Constable	7 September	IRA	Killed in landmine explosion near Pomeroy

		1981 continued		
Victim Name	Rank	Murdered	Murdered By	Method Of Murder
Proctor, John	R/Constable	14 September	IRA	Off duty, he was visiting his wife who had just given birth in the Mid Ulster Hospital, Magherafelt, when he was shot dead
Stewart, George	Constable	26 September	IRA	Off duty, he was fatally wounded in a gun attack at Main Street, Killough, Co Down.
Beck, Alexander	Constable	28 September	IRA	Fatally wounded when his Land Rover was hit by a rocket at Suffolk Road, Belfast
Lyttle, Silas	R/Constable	17 November	IRA	Off duty, he was fatally wounded in gun attack outside his home in Grange, Ballygawley
Coulter, William	Constable	28 November	IRA	Fatally wounded by booby trap bomb at Unity Flats, Belfast

			1982	
Victim Name	**Rank**	**Murdered**	**Murdered By**	**Method Of Murder**
Duddy, Norman	Inspector	28 March	IRA	Fatally wounded in gun attack as he and his sons left Strand Road Presbyterian Church, Londonderry
Brown, David	Sergeant	16 April	IRA	Fatally wounded in gun attack at Springfield Crescent, Belfast
Caskey, Samuel	Constable	4 May	IRA	Fatally wounded in gun attack at the Diamond, Londonderry
Reeves, David	D/Constable	11 June	IRA	Killed by booby trap bomb at Shantallow, Londonderry
Eagleson, John	R/Constable	1 October	IRA	Fatally wounded in gun attack on way to his civilian employment in Upper Kildress Road, Cookstown
Crothers, Charles	R/Constable	5 October	IRA	Fatally wounded in gun attack at his civilian employment at Altnagelvin, Londonderry
Hamilton, Paul	Constable	27 October	IRA	Killed by bomb at Kinnego Embankment, Lurgan
McCloy, Alan	Constable	27 October	IRA	Killed by bomb at Kinnego Embankment, Lurgan
Quinn, John	Sergeant	27 October	IRA	Killed by bomb at Kinnego Embankment, Lurgan
Ewing, Gary	Constable	9 November	IRA	Off duty, he was fatally wounded when a booby trap bomb exploded under his car near Lakeland Forum, Enniskillen
Corkey, Snowdon	R/Constable	16 November	INLA	Fatally wounded in gun attack in Newry Street, Markethill
Irwin, Ronald	R/Constable	16 November	INLA	Fatally wounded in gun attack in Newry Street, Markethill

		1983		
Victim Name	**Rank**	**Murdered**	**Murdered By**	**Method Of Murder**
Brown, Eric	Sergeant	6 January	IRA	Fatally wounded in gun attack at the Square, Rostrevor
Quinn, Brian	R/Constable	6 January	IRA	Fatally wounded in gun attack at the Square, Rostrevor
Olphert, John	R/Constable	18 January	IRA	Was serving customers in his shop at Sperrin Park, Londonderry when he was shot dead by gunmen
Magill, Edward	R/Constable	20 February	IRA	Fatally wounded in gun attack at Warrenpoint RUC Station
Wilson, Gordon	Sergeant	21 February	IRA	Fatally injured by booby trap bomb at Lower English Street, Armagh
McCormack, Lindsay	Constable	2 March	IRA	Fatally wounded in gun attack at Serpentine Road, Belfast
Morton, Frederick	R/Constable	15 March	IRA	Was driving his bread van at Portadown Road, Newry when he was fatally wounded in gun attack
Cathcart, Gerald	Constable	16 May	IRA	Fatally wounded in gun attack at Linkview Park, Belfast
Carson, Colin	R/Constable	26 May	INLA	Fatally wounded in gun attack at Molesworth Estate, Cookstown
Wasson, John	Constable	7 September	INLA	Fatally wounded in gun attack outside his home at Cathedral Road, Armagh
Ferguson, James	R/Constable	6 October	IRA	Fatally wounded in gun attack at Meadowlands Estate, Downpatrick
Finlay, William	R/Constable	6 October	IRA	Fatally wounded in gun attack at Meadowlands Estate, Downpatrick
Hallawell, John	Constable	28 October	IRA	Fatally wounded in gun attack at Sheelin Park, Shantallow, Londonderry
Clarke, Paul	Constable	1 November	IRA	Fatally injured in mortar attack at Carrickmore RUC Station
Fyfe, Stephen	Sergeant	4 November	IRA	Fatally wounded by a bomb as he attended a lecture at the Ulster Polytechnic, Jordanstown

1983 continued				
Victim Name	*Rank*	*Murdered*	*Murdered By*	*Method Of Murder*
Martin, John	Inspector	4 November	IRA	Fatally wounded by a bomb as he attended a lecture at the Ulster Polytechnic, Jordanstown
McFadden, John	R/Constable	5 November	IRA	Fatally wounded in gun attack outside his home in Rasharkin
Fitzpatrick, William	R/Constable	10 November	IRA	Fatally wounded in gun attack at his home near Kilkeel

1984				
Victim Name	*Rank*	*Murdered*	*Murdered By*	*Method Of Murder*
Fullerton, William	R/Constable	10 January	IRA	Fatally wounded in gun attack at Greenbank Roundabout outside Newry
Bingham, Thomas	Constable	31 January	IRA	Killed by landmine on the Newry/Forkhill Road
Savage, William	Sergeant	31 January	IRA	Killed by a landmine on the Newry/Forkhill Road
Dawson, Michael	Constable	12 April	Loyalists	Killed by booby trap bomb at University Street, Belfast
Elliott, Trevor	R/Constable	18 May	IRA	Fatally injured in landmine explosion on the Camlough/Crossmaglen Road
Gray, Neville	Constable	18 May	IRA	Fatally injured in landmine explosion on the Camlough/Crossmaglen Road
Todd, Michael	Constable	15 June	INLA	Fatally wounded in gun attack at Lenadoon Avenue, Belfast
White, Malcolm	Sergeant	12 August	IRA	Fatally injured by landmine on Gortin/Greencastle Road
McDonald, William	Sergeant	4 November	IRA	Died as a result of injuries sustained in bomb attack at the Ulster Polytechnic 1983

		1985		
Victim Name	*Rank*	*Murdered*	*Murdered By*	*Method Of Murder*
Campbell, Geoffrey	R/Constable	28 February	IRA	Fatally wounded in mortar attack on Newry RUC Station
Donaldson, Alexander	C/Constable	28 February	IRA	Fatally wounded in mortar attack on Newry RUC Station
Dowd, John	Sergeant	28 February	IRA	Fatally wounded in mortar attack on Newry RUC Station
Kelly, Ivy	Constable	28 February	IRA	Fatally wounded in mortar attack on Newry RUC Station
McFerran, Paul	R/Constable	28 February	IRA	Fatally wounded in mortar attack on Newry RUC Station
McGookin, Rosemary	Constable	28 February	IRA	Fatally wounded in mortar attack on Newry RUC Station
McHenry, Sean	R/Constable	28 February	IRA	Fatally wounded in mortar attack on Newry RUC Station
Price, Denis	R/Constable	28 February	IRA	Fatally wounded in mortar attack on Newry RUC Station
Topping, David	Constable	28 February	IRA	Fatally wounded in mortar attack on Newry RUC Station
McCormack, Hugh	Sergeant	3 March	IRA	Fatally wounded in gun attack as he and his family attended Mass in Enniskillen
Bell, John	R/Constable	29 March	IRA	Fatally wounded in gun attack in Rathfriland
Kay, Michael	R/Constable	3 April	IRA	Killed by booby trap outside Newry Courthouse
Baird, David	Constable	20 May	IRA	Killed by bomb at Killeen Customs post
Doak, Tracey	Constable	20 May	IRA	Killed by bomb at Killeen Customs post
Rodgers, Steven	R/Constable	20 May	IRA	Killed by bomb at Killeen Customs post
Wilson, William	Inspector	20 May	IRA	Killed by bomb at Killeen Customs post
Murphy, Francis	Sergeant	21 May	IRA	Fatally wounded in gun attack as he dropped school children at Drumsallon Primary School

1985 continued				
Victim Name	Rank	Murdered	Murdered By	Method Of Murder
Agnew, William	R/Constable	16 June	IRA	Off duty, he was fatally wounded in gun attack as he sat in his car with his fiancée in Kilrea, Co Londonderry
Gilliland, William	Constable	18 June	IRA	Fatally wounded by bomb at Kinawley Road, Co Fermanagh
Vance, Martin	Inspector	31 August	IRA	Off duty, he was fatally wounded in gun attack at Crossgar, Co Down
Hanson, David	Constable	15 November	IRA	Killed by landmine explosion at Castleblaney Road, Crossmaglen
Clements, William	R/Constable	7 December	IRA	Fatally wounded in gun attack on Ballygawley RUC Station
Gilliland, George	Constable	7 December	IRA	Fatally wounded in gun attack on Ballygawley RUC Station

1986				
Victim Name	Rank	Murdered	Murdered By	Method Of Murder
McCandless, James	Constable	1 January	IRA	Killed by bomb at Ogle Street, Armagh
Williams, Michael	R/Constable	1 January	IRA	Killed by bomb at Ogle Street, Armagh
Breen, Derek	D/Constable	11 February	IRA	Fatally wounded in gun attack in Maguirebridge, Co Fermanagh
Hazlett, James	Inspector	23 April	IRA	Fatally wounded in gun attack outside his home in Newcastle, Co Down
McBride, David	Constable	22 May	IRA	Killed by a bomb at Larkin's Road, Crossmaglen
Smyth, William	Constable	22 May	IRA	Killed by a bomb at Larkin's Road, Crossmaglen
McVitty, John	A/Constable	8 July	IRA	Fatally injured in gun attack as he cut bushes on his farm at Drumady, Rosslea, Co Fermanagh
Allen, Charles	Constable	26 July	IRA	Fatally injured in gun attack in Market Square, Newry
Blackbourne, Karl	Constable	26 July	IRA	Fatally injured in gun attack in Market Square, Newry
Kilpatrick, Peter	Sergeant	26 July	IRA	Fatally injured in gun attack in Market Square, Newry

1986 continued				
Victim Name	*Rank*	*Murdered*	*Murdered By*	*Method Of Murder*
Dobbin, Desmond	R/Constable	12 October	IRA	Fatally injured in mortar attack on New Barnsley RUC Station
Patterson, Derek	Constable	10 November	IRA	Fatally wounded in gun attack at Fitzroy Avenue, Belfast

1987				
Victim Name	*Rank*	*Murdered*	*Murdered By*	*Method Of Murder*
Crawford, Ivan	R/Constable	9 January	IRA	Fatally wounded in bomb explosion in centre of Enniskillen
Nesbitt, Peter	R/Constable	10 March	IRA	Fatally wounded in bomb explosion at Ardoyne, Belfast
Bennison, John	D/Sergeant	23 March	IRA	Killed in booby trap explosion at Magee College, Londonderry
Wilson, Austin	D/Inspector	23 March	IRA	Killed in booby trap explosion at Magee College, Londonderry
Shaw, George	R/Constable	3 April	IRA	Fatally wounded in gun attack on Ballynahinch RUC Station
Armstrong, Frederick	R/Constable	11 April	IRA	Fatally wounded in gun attack at Portrush
McLean, Robert	R/Constable	11 April	IRA	Fatally wounded in gun attack at Portrush
Ead, David	Inspector	20 April	IRA	Fatally injured in gun attack outside Newcastle RUC Station
Cooke, Thomas	Sergeant	23 April	IRA	Fatally wounded in gun attack as he left his golf club in Londonderry
McLean, Sam	Constable	2 June	IRA	Fatally wounded in gun attack as he worked on the farm of his elderly parents in Drumbreen, Co Donegal
Guthrie, Robert	Sergeant	23 June	IRA	Fatally wounded in gun attack outside Antrim Road RUC Station
Kennedy, Norman	Constable	26 July	IRA	Shot dead in his Ballymena home as he watched television with his wife
Carson, Ernest	D/Constable	26 August	IRA	Fatally wounded in gun attack in docks area of Belfast

Victim Name	Rank	Murdered	Murdered By	Method Of Murder
1987 continued				
Malone, Michael	D/Constable	26 August	IRA	Fatally wounded in gun attack in docks area of Belfast
Finlay, Winston	R/Constable	30 August	IRA	Was getting out of his car driven by his wife outside his home near Magherafelt when he was shot dead by gunmen
Armstrong, Edward	R/Constable	8 November	IRA	Killed in the Enniskillen Poppy Day bomb

Victim Name	Rank	Murdered	Murdered By	Method Of Murder
1988				
Gilmore, Colin	R/Constable	25 January	IRA	Fatally wounded in drogue bomb attack at Falls Road, Belfast
Graham, Clive	Constable	21 March	IRA	Fatally wounded in gun attack in Creggan, Londonderry
Warnock, John	D/Constable	2 August	IRA	Killed by booby trap bomb near Lisburn RUC Station
Lamour, John	Constable	11 October	IRA	Shot dead as he worked in his brother's ice cream shop on the Lisburn Road, Belfast
McCrone, Hugh	R/Constable	26 October	IRA	Fatally wounded in gun attack near Kinawley, Co Fermanagh
Monteith, William	R/Constable	21 November	IRA	Fatally wounded in gun attack at town barrier in Castlederg

Victim Name	Rank	Murdered	Murdered By	Method Of Murder
1989				
Montgomery, Stephen	Constable	28 January	IRA	Fatally wounded in drogue bomb attack at Melmont Road, Sion Mills
Breen, Harry	C/Supt.	20 March	IRA	Fatally wounded in gun attack at Jonesborough as he returned from Dundalk Garda Station
Buchannan, Robert	Supt.	20 March	IRA	Fatally wounded in gun attack at Jonesborough as he returned from Dundalk Garda Station

1989 continued				
Victim Name	*Rank*	*Murdered*	*Murdered By*	*Method Of Murder*
Black, David	R/Constable	27 June	IRA	Fatally wounded by booby trap bomb under his car in Londonderry
Annett, Norman	Constable	1 July	IRA	Fatally injured in gun attack on his mother's home in Garvagh
Bell, Alexander	R/Constable	24 July	IRA	Fatally injured in bomb attack between Waterfoot and Cushendall
Harris, Alwyn	Supt.	8 October	IRA	Fatally injured by booby trap bomb under his car as he and his wife travelled to church
Marshall, Michael	Constable	20 October	IRA	Fatally wounded in gun attack in Belleek

1990				
Victim Name	*Rank*	*Murdered*	*Murdered By*	*Method Of Murder*
Monteith, Derek	Inspector	22 January	IRA	Fatally wounded in gun attack on his home in Armagh
Starrett, George	R/Constable	28 March	IRA	Fatally wounded in gun attack on his home in Armagh
Beckett, Harry	Constable	30 June	IRA	Fatally wounded in gun attack in Queen Street/Castle Street, Belfast
Meyer, Gary	Constable	30 June	IRA	Fatally wounded in gun attack in Queen Street/Castle Street, Belfast
Hanson, William	Constable	24 July	IRA	Killed in landmine explosion between Armagh and Caledon, Co Armagh
Sterritt, David	R/Constable	24 July	IRA	Killed in landmine explosion between Armagh and Caledon, Co Armagh
Wills, Cyril	R/Constable	24 July	IRA	Killed in landmine explosion between Armagh and Caledon, Co Armagh
Robinson, Louis	D/Constable	16 September	IRA	Abducted as he travelled back across the border after a fishing trip to the south. His body was found two days later near Killeen, Co Armagh.

Victim Name	Rank	Murdered	Murdered By	Method Of Murder
Todd, Samuel	Constable	15 October	IRA	Fatally wounded in gun attack in High Street, Belfast
Murphy, David	D/Inspector	10 November	IRA	Fatally wounded in a gun attack on the shore of Lough Neagh
Taylor, Thomas	R/Constable	10 November	IRA	Fatally wounded in a gun attack on the shore of Lough Neagh
Wethers, Wilfred	R/Constable	20 December	IRA	Fatally wounded in gun attack at Banbridge Road, Lurgan

1991				
Victim Name	Rank	Murdered	Murdered By	Method Of Murder
McGarry, Spence	D/Constable	6 April	IRA	Killed by booby trap bomb under his car in Ballycastle, Co Antrim
McCrum, Samuel	Sergeant	13 April	IRA	Fatally wounded in gun attack in Lisburn, Co Antrim
Gillespie, Stephen	Sergeant	2 May	IRA	Fatally wounded in gun and rocket attack in West Belfast
Carrothers, Douglas	R/Constable	17 May	IRA	Killed by booby trap bomb under his car at driveway of his home in Lisbellaw, Co Fermanagh
Spence, Edward	Constable	26 May	IRA	Fatally wounded in gun attack at Lower Crescent, Belfast
Clarke, Erik	Constable	17 September	IRA	Fatally wounded in rocket attack in Swatragh, Co Londonderry

1992				
Victim Name	Rank	Murdered	Murdered By	Method Of Murder
McMurray, Colleen	Constable	28 March	IRA	Fatally wounded in mortar attack on Newry RUC Station
Douglas, James	Constable	10 October	IRA	Off duty, he was shot dead in gun attack in Belfast City Centre.
Corbett, Alan	R/Constable	15 November	IRA	Fatally wounded in gun attack in Main Street, Belcoo

1993				
Victim Name	**Rank**	**Murdered**	**Murdered By**	**Method Of Murder**
Ferguson, Michael	Constable	23 January	IRA	Fatally wounded in gun attack at Richmond Centre, Londonderry
Williamson, Reginald	Constable	24 February	IRA	Killed by booby trap bomb under his car near Moy, Co Tyrone
Reid, Jonathan	Constable	25 March	IRA	Shot dead by sniper in Crossmaglen, Co Armagh
Woods, Brian	R/Constable	2 November	IRA	Shot dead by sniper near Newry RUC Station
Beacom, William	Constable	12 December	IRA	Fatally wounded in gun attack in Fivemiletown, Co Fermanagh
Smyth, Ernest	R/Constable	12 December	IRA	Fatally wounded in gun attack in Fivemiletown, Co Fermanagh

1994				
Victim Name	**Rank**	**Murdered**	**Murdered By**	**Method Of Murder**
Beacom, Johnston	Constable	17 February	IRA	Killed in rocket attack in Markets area of Belfast
Haggan, Jackie	Constable	12 March	IRA	Shot dead while having a drink with his wife at Dunmore Greyhound Stadium
Pollock, Gregory	Constable	20 April	IRA	Killed in mortar attack in Spencer Road, Londonderry

1995				
Victim Name	**Rank**	**Murdered**	**Murdered By**	**Method Of Murder**
Seymour, Jim	Constable	2 March	IRA	Died having been in a coma for 22 years following a gun attack on Coalisland RUC Station on 4 May 1973

1997				
Victim Name	Rank	Murdered	Murdered By	Method Of Murder
Bradshaw, Darren	Constable	9 May	IRA	Off duty, he was shot dead in city centre bar in Belfast.
Taylor, Greg	Constable	1 June	Loyalists	Beaten to death outside bar in Ballymoney
Graham, John	Constable	16 June	IRA	Shot dead while on patrol in Lurgan town centre
Johnston, David	R/Constable	16 June	IRA	Shot dead while on patrol in Lurgan town centre

1998				
Victim Name	Rank	Murdered	Murdered By	Method Of Murder
O'Reilly, Frank	Constable	6 October	Loyalists	Fatally injured in blast bomb attack in Corcrain Estate, Portadown

Ulster Defence Regiment
Roll of Honour

1971		
Date of Murder	*Victim's Name*	*Place of Murder*
9 August	Pte. Winston Donnell	Claudy
3 September	Pte. Frank Veitch	Kinawley RUC Station
1 December	Pte. Dennis Wilson	Caledon, Curlough
8 December	Pte. Sean Russell	New Barnsley, West Belfast
10 December	Sgt. Kenneth Smyth	Clady

1972		
Date of Murder	*Victim's Name*	*Place of Murder*
13 January	Sgt. Maynard Crawford	Newtownabbey
16 February	Pte. Thomas Callaghan	Creggan, Londonderry
29 February	Sgt. Harry Dickson	Lurgan
1 March	Pte. Tommy Fletcher	Belleck
4 March	Capt. Marcus McCausland	Creggan, Londonderry
8 March	L/Cpl. Joseph Jardine	Middletown
20 March	Pte. Samuel Trainor	Lower Donegal Rd. Belfast
19 April	Cpl. James Elliot	Newtownhamilton
20 May	L/Cpl. William Gillespie	Dungannon
9 June	Cpl. Ray Stanton	Belfast
9 June	Pte. Edward Megahey	Londonderry
13 July	Pte. Harry Russell	East Belfast
22 July	Pte. Robert McComb	Crumlin Road, Belfast
7 August	L/Cpl. Harry Creighton	Newtownbutler
25 August	L/Cpl. A. Johnston	Enniskillen
25 August	Pte. J. Eames	Enniskillen
6 September	L/Cpl. Victor Smyth	Portadown
21 September	Pte. Thomas Bullock	Derrlin, Killynick
10 October	C/Sgt. John Ruddy	Newry
14 October	Pte. T. G. Maguire	Belfast
22 October	Pte. Rokin Bell	Newtownbutler
8 November	2nd Lt. Irwin Long	Lurgan
22 November	Pte. Samuel Porter	Maghera
5 December	Pte. William Bogle	Castlederg
15 December	Pte. F. D. Greeves	Moy Road, Armagh
20 December	Pte. George Hamilton	Londonderry

1973		
Date of Murder	*Victim's Name*	*Place of Murder*
4 January	Capt. James Hood	Stradarren, Claudy
16 January	Cpl. David Bingham	Lower Falls, West Belfast
3 March	Sgt. David Deacon	Mullenan, Londonderry
16 March	Pte. William Kenny	New Lodge, Belfast
10 May	Cpl. Frank Caddoo	Aughnacloy
20 July	Pte. S. Watt	Newtownhamilton
28 August	Pte. Kenneth Hill	Armagh
7 September	Pte. Matthew Lilly	Belcoo
16 October	Pte. Tommy Forsythe	Belfast

1974		
Date of Murder	*Victim's Name*	*Place of Murder*
17 January	Pte. Robert Jameson	Fintona Trillick
19 January	Capt. Cormac McCabe	Clougher
3 March	Cpl. Robert Moffett	Dunnamore, Cookstown
11 April	WO2 Harold Sunnamon	Dungannon
2 May	Pte. Eva Martin	Clougher
23 July	Cpl. John Conley	Garvagh
17 November	Pte. John McCready	High Street, Newry

1975		
Date of Murder	*Victim's Name*	*Place of Murder*
3 June	Sgt. Alfred Doyle	Killan
30 August	Cpl. James Frazer	Newtownhamilton
31 August	L/Cpl. Joseph Reid	Armagh
6 November	L/Cpl. John Bell	Newtownhamilton
10 November	C/Sgt. John Nesbitt	Keady
25 November	Pte. Robert Stott	Fountain Estate, Londonderry

1976		
Date of Murder	*Victim's Name*	*Place of Murder*
22 January	Pte. John Arrell	Clady
25 January	David McDowell	Middletown
26 February	Pte. Joe McCullough	Newtownhamilton
1 April	Pte. John McCutcheon	Toomebridge
2 April	S/Sgt. Henry Lennox	Rocktown, Maghera
5 April	Capt. William McConnell	Middletown
6 April	L/Cpl. Jean Leggett	Middletown
29 April	Pte. Edward Stewart	Dungannon
30 July	Pte. Robert Scott	Coagh
26 October	Lt. Joseph Wilson	Armagh

1976 continued		
Date of Murder	*Victim's Name*	*Place of Murder*
28 October	L/Cpl. Stanley Adams	Pomeroy
7 November	Capt. William R. Bond	Londonderry
9 November	L/Cpl. Joe Speero	Desertmartin
11 November	L/Cpl. W. C. McCaughey	Boveedy, Kilrea
15 November	Pte. George Lutton	Lurgan
18 November	Cpl. William Kidd	Londonderry

1977		
Date of Murder	*Victim's Name*	*Place of Murder*
23 February	Maj. Peter Hill	Londonderry
9 March	John Reid	Gaslough, Caledon
15 March	David McQuillan	Bellaghy
25 March	Cpl. David Graham	Coalisland
6 April	L/Cpl Gerald Cloete	Cloughglass
29 April	Capt. Walter Shiello	Dungannon
10 May	Cpl. James Geddis	North Belfast
8 June	L/Cpl Gerald Tucker	RVH West Belfast
27 July	Cpl. James McFall	Belfast
8 September	Cpl. Hugh Rogers	Dunmurry
13 September	2nd Lt. George Smyrl	Drumlee Bridge, Gortin
24 September	George Bloomer	Dungannon
8 October	Margaret Hearst	Tynan
2 November	2nd Lt. William Kerr	Magherafelt

1978		
Date of Murder	*Victim's Name*	*Place of Murder*
12 January	Cpl. Cecil Grillo	Newry
7 February	Sgt. John Eaglesham	Rock, Cookstown
8 February	Cpl. William Gordon	Maghera
14 April	Cpl. William McKee	Omagh
25 June	Pte. Alan Ferguson	Belcoo
6 October	Capt. Charles Henning	Patrick Street, Newry
27 November	Sgt. Robert Batchelor	West Belfast

1979		
Date of Murder	*Victim's Name*	*Place of Murder*
15 March	Pte. Robert McNally	Portadown
13 April	L/Cpl. Tommy Armstrong	Tynan
25 April	Pte. John Graham	Seskimore, Omagh
29 April	Pte. George S. Gibson	Edendork, Dungannon
6 June	Pte. Alexander Gore	South Belfast
19 June	Pte. John Hannigan	Omagh
24 June	Pte. James J. Porter	Mountmorris, Glenanne

1979 continued		
Date of Murder	Victim's Name	Place of Murder
15 October	Cpl. Herbert Kennaghan	Rosslea
19 October	Pte. A. Robinson	Kilcootry, Fintona
30 October	Cpl. Fred H. Irwin	Dungannon

1980		
Date of Murder	Victim's Name	Place of Murder
6 January	Pte. Richard Wilson	Burren Bridge, Castlewellan
6 January	Pte. Roy Smith	Burren Bridge, Castlewellan
6 January	Pte. James Cochrane	Burren Bridge, Castlewellan
5 February	L/Cpl. A. A. Abercombe	Kinewley
7 June	Pte. William Latimer	Newtownbutler
3 August	Pte. William John Clarke	Pettigo
10 October	Pte. Marcus J. Hewitt	Portadown
25 November	Pte. Norman Donaldson	Derrygonnelly
10 December	Pte. Colin Quinn	Belfast

1981		
Date of Murder	Victim's Name	Place of Murder
16 January	Maj. William Toombs	Warrenpoint
10 February	L/Cpl. Sam Montgomery	Londonderry
27 March	Pte. David Smith	Belfast
16 April	Pte. John Donnelly	Moy
28 April	L/Cpl Richard McKee	Warrenpoint
25 May	Pte. Thomas Ritchie	Magherafelt
5 June	L/Cpl. Ronnie Graham	Lisnaskea
12 September	Pte. Alan Clarke	Maghera
29 September	Pte. Mark Stockman	Mackeys, West Belfast
21 October	Sgt. Julian Connelly	Glengormley
11 November	Pte. Cecil Graham	Donagh, Lisnaskea
17 November	Cpl. Thomas Beacon	Lisnaskea
19 November	L/Cpl. John McKeegan	Londonderry

1982		
Date of Murder	Victim's Name	Place of Murder
8 January	Pte. Stephen Carleton	North Belfast
27 April	Lt. James Hamilton	Londonderry
15 June	Pte. Hugh Cummings	Strabane
7 October	L/Cpl. Fred Williamson	Armagh
29 October	Sgt. Thomas Cochrane	Lislea, Bessbrook
10 November	Cpl. Charles Spence	Armagh
20 December	Cpl. Austin Smith	Armagh

1983		
Date of Murder	*Victim's Name*	*Place of Murder*
25 February	L/Cpl. Cecil McNeill	Dungannon
4 June	Pte. Andrew Stinson	Dungannon
13 July	Pte. John Roxborough	Ballymacilroy Hill, Ballygawley
13 July	Pte. Ronald Alexander	Ballymacilroy Hill, Ballygawley
13 July	Pte. Oswell Neely	Ballymacilroy Hill, Ballygawley
13 July	Cpl. Thomas Harron	Ballymacilroy Hill, Ballygawley
23 August	Cpl. Ronald Finlay	Strabane
24 October	Pte. Cyrus T. Campbell	Dungannon
14 November	Maj. Charles Armstrong	Armagh
17 December	L/Cpl. Brown V. McKeown	Maghera

1984		
Date of Murder	*Victim's Name*	*Place of Murder*
2 January	Pte. Robert G. Elliott	Castlederg, Strabane
20 January	Pte. Linden Houston	Dunmurry
2 March	L/Cpl. Thomas Loughlin	Castlederg
8 March	Pte. David Montgomery	Moira
8 May	Pte. Johnston	Drumglass Hospital, Dungannon
12 May	C/Sgt. Ivan Hillen	Lismore, Augher
4 June	Pte. David Chambers	Dollingstown
14 July	Cpl. Heather Kerrigan	Castlederg
14 July	Pte. Norman McKinley	Castlederg
7 September	Pte. Robert D. Bennett	Dungannon

1985		
Date of Murder	*Victim's Name*	*Place of Murder*
1 February	Pte. James Graham	Derrylin, Enniskillen
28 February	Pte. T. W. Harkness	Pomeroy
18 November	Sgt. R. F. Boyd	Londonderry
29 November	Capt. G. Hanna	Kilkeel

1986		
Date of Murder	*Victim's Name*	*Place of Murder*
15 January	Pte. W. V. Foster	Castlederg
3 February	Pte. J. F. Early	Belcoo
26 March	Pte. Thomas Irwin	Omagh
8 April	Pte. W. C. Pollock	Castlederg
28 May	Cpl. David Brown	Kilkeel
28 May	Oliver (Search Dog)	Kilkeel
1 July	Pte. D. W. Hill	Drumnaness, Downpatrick
4 August	Sgt. D. M. Taggart	Belfast
6 October	Pte. Martin A. Blaney	Dungannon

1987		
Date of Murder	*Victim's Name*	*Place of Murder*
26 January	Maj. George Shaw	Dungannon
3 April	Cpl. T. J. Oldman	Edemy, Enniskillen
25 April	Pte. William Graham	Pomeroy
21 May	Capt. I. R. Anderson	Carrickmore
12 June	Pte. J. J. McIlwaine	Dunmurry
26 June	Pte. G. J. Tracey	Belfast
23 July	Pte. W. R. Megrath	Belfast
17 September	Pte. S. W. Megrath	Belfast

1988		
Date of Murder	*Victim's Name*	*Place of Murder*
16 January	Pte. W. J. R. Stewart	Dungannon
16 January	Capt. T. D. Armstrong	Belfast
15 February	L/Cpl. Alan Johnston	Kilkeel
24 February	Pte. Freddie Starrett	Royal Ave, Central Belfast
24 February	Pte. James Cummings	Royal Ave, Central Belfast
6 April	Cpl. W. T. Burleigh	Derrylin
26 April	Pte. E. Gibson	Ardboe, Coagh
4 June	L/Cpl. Michael Darcy	Castlederg
2 August	L/Cpl. Roy Butler	Park Centre, West Belfast
3 August	Pte. Raymond McNicholl	Cookstown
25 September	Pte. Stephen McKinney	Armagh
16 December	Pte. John Moreland	Ardpatrick Ave, Downpatrick

1989		
Date of Murder	*Victim's Name*	*Place of Murder*
14 March	Pte. Hardy	Dungannon
17 November	L/Cpl. David Halligan	Armagh

1990		
Date of Murder	*Victim's Name*	*Place of Murder*
8 March	Sgt. Thomas Jamison	Tullynure, Magherafelt
9 April	Pte. John Birch	Ballyduggan Road, Downpatrick
9 April	Pte. Michael Adams	Ballyduggan Road, Downpatrick
9 April	Pte. Steven Smart	Ballyduggan Road, Downpatrick
9 April	L/Cpl. John Bradley	Ballyduggan Road, Downpatrick
23 September	Pte. Colin McCullough	Oxford Island, Lurgan
2 November	WO2 Albert Cooper	Union Street, Cookstown

1991		
Date of Murder	*Victim's Name*	*Place of Murder*
1 March	Pte. Roger Love	Killyrea Road, Armagh
1 March	Pte. Paul Sutcliffe	Killylea Road, Armagh
31 May	Pte. Robert Bleakley	Glenanne
31 May	L/Cpl. Bobby Crozier	Glenanne
31 May	Pte. Sidney Hamilton	Glenanne
17 June	Pte. Brian Lawrence	Drumcrue Street, North Belfast
6 November	Pte. Michael Boxall	Bellaghy
26 November	L/Cpl. Ken Newell	Cregganduff, Crossmaglen

Ulster Defence Regiment
Ex-Members

Below is a list of ex-members of the regiment that have been murdered.

1971	D. J. McCormick
1972	I. Scott
1973	J. I. Vennard
1974	G. W. Saunderston • W. D. J. Hutchinson
1975	G. McCall
1976	N. Campbell • K. Worton • W. J. Freeburn
1977	R. J. Harrison
1978	M. Riley • G. Johnston
1979	S. Wray • A. Dunne • R. G. Hawthorne • J. Fowler • R. A. Lockhart
1980	A. Lundy • R. V. Morrow • W. G. Elliott
1981	J. Robinson • J. Proctor • H. R. Hall • C. D. Neville • J. McClintock
1982	N. Hanna • T. C. I. Cunningham • W. Ilveen • J. Eagleson
1982	D. Crothers • S. Corkey • R. Irwin • J. Gibson
1983	J. R. E. Truckle
1984	R. A. Funston • H. Gallagher • M. Simpson
1985	G. Campbell • J. D. McElhinney • D. P. Topping
1986	H. McConville
1987	N. Cush • W. C. Finlay • H. Henry • C. Watson
1989	J. R. Glover • J. Griffiths
1990	D. Sterritt • D. M. Pollock • N. Kendall • H. B. Gilmore
1991	W. J. E. Boyd • R. M. A. Finlay
1993	D. H. Martin • J. Lyness • J. A. Burns
1994	S. W. E. Smyth • M. A. Smyth
2002	David Caldwell